STUFFED CAPSICUMS (see page 16)

SEMOLINA CAKES WITH BUTTER AND CHEESE (see page 71)

ITALIAN COOKBOOK

[Though our author is no stranger to Rome and the provinces, Alitalia Airline graciously invited Margaret Fulton to return there to review the very latest trends in Italian cookery. The airline itself is renown for its fine Italian food and we would like to thank Alitalia for its generous gesture. Our book is that much better for it. *The publisher.*]

Published by Paul Hamlyn Pty Ltd
176 South Creek Road,
Dee Why West,
New South Wales, 2099
First published 1973
Copyright Paul Hamlyn Pty Ltd 1973
Printed in Hong Kong
Registry number 0 600 07076 X

EDITOR: ELIZABETH SEWELL
PHOTOGRAPHER: REG MORRISON
DESIGNER: DOMINIQUE CLARKE

ITALIAN COOKBOOK

H_G

PAUL HAMLYN
Sydney London New York Toronto

INTRODUCTION

Wherever you go in Italy whether it be an inexpensive trattoria or a luxurious restaurant the food and atmosphere will always be enjoyable. In homes it is the same, even family meals assume a party air.

Italian cooking is lighthearted and imaginative and there is very little difference between the cooking of the poor and that of the rich. Nearly everybody from a Sicilian worker to the Florentine aristocrat likes to start a meal with pasta and end with fruit and cheese. Maybe nowadays only the rich can afford scampi from the Adriatic, truffles from Piedmont or beef from Tuscany but the poor enjoy their canneloni as much as the rich enjoy their beef, and as all Italians know, what does it matter as long as you enjoy what you eat.

The best Italian dishes are simple like Milan's risotto cooked with saffron and risi bisi of Venice, a soup of rice, fresh green peas and ham or golden semolina gnocchi gilded with butter and parmesan.

Pasta is as Italian as opera and as varied. There is said to be about 400 varieties of pasta from the whispy 'capelli d'angelo' (angels' hair) to broad, flat lasagne and the giant canneloni (large pipes). Pasta comes in all shapes too, little bows, stars, alphabets, small shells, big shells. Some varieties are eaten with a sauce, sometimes just butter, others are stuffed with meat, cheese, spices and herbs. One word of warning, pasta should be cooked 'al dente' (to the tooth), that is to say it should be removed from the boiling water while still firm to the bite. Pasta is meant to be chewed, not swallowed like a soft pudding.

Many dishes are flavoured with herbs — basil, oregano, rosemary, and the pungent Italian parsley which you can grow in your garden or even a window box. Use only the best quality Italian olive oil. Olives, anchovies and a little garlic, wine and cheese are used with discretion and tomatoes feature in many dishes. But for truly authentic flavour in your Italian dishes look for the speciality ingredients in a good delicatessen or the gourmet section of large retail stores. Some just can't be substituted, for example, cheddar for Parmesan or Mozzarella. And when using grating cheese like Parmesan or Romano buy it in wedges and grate it as you need it. Italian rice is available and pasta from Naples, try the Italian artichokes in oil or brine and when fresh tomatoes are expensive seek out the Italian canned variety or the tomato pastes. Look too for Italian wines. This is not to say that local products are not good but it is interesting to taste the Italian product.

Italian cooking is good cooking and best of all it is fun cooking. It seems that my own home takes on a festive air every time I prepare Italian food. We relax and there is laughter and song in our hearts. I hope you find it this way too. Buono Gusto

CONTENTS

GUIDE TO WEIGHTS AND MEASURES

Because of the introduction of the metric system to Australia, we give both metric and imperial weights and measures for all ingredients.

IMPERIAL GUIDE

Weight and Volume Measures

The imperial weights and measures used throughout this book refer to those adopted by the Standards Association of Australia (A.S. S2-1970 Measuring Cups and Spoons for Domestic Purposes). All spoon measurements are level unless otherwise stated. A good set of imperial scales, a graduated Australian Standard 8 fl oz measuring cup and a set of Australian Standard measuring spoons will be most helpful.

The Australian Standard measuring cup has a capacity of 8 fluid ounces.

The Australian Standard tablespoon has a capacity of 20 millilitres.

The Australian Standard teaspoon has a capacity of 5 millilitres.

The British imperial pint (used in Australia) has a volume of 20 fluid ounces.

AMERICAN/CANADIAN WEIGHTS

American weights and measures are the same except for the tablespoon and the pint.

Housewives in AMERICA and CANADA using this book should remember that the Australian standard measuring tablespoon has a capacity of 20 millilitres, whereas the AMERICAN/CANADIAN standard measuring tablespoon has a capacity of 15 millilitres, therefore all tablespoon measures should be taken generously in AMERICA and CANADA.

It is also important to know that the imperial pint (20 fluid ounces) is used in Australia, whereas the AMERICAN/CANADIAN pint has a volume of 16 fluid ounces.

METRIC GUIDE

Weight and Volume Measures

The metric weights and measures used throughout this book refer to those adopted by the Standards Association of Australia (AS 1325 1972 Metric

Measuring Cups and Spoons and Standard Litre Measure for Domestic Purposes). All spoon measurements are level unless otherwise stated. A good set of metric scales, an Australian Standard litre measure, a graduated Australian Standard metric measuring cup and a set of Australian Standard metric measuring spoons will be most helpful.

The Australian Standard litre measure has a capacity of 4 metric measuring cups.

The Australian Standard metric measuring cup has a capacity of 250 millilitres.

The Australian Standard metric tablespoon has a capacity of 20 millilitres.

The Australian Standard metric teaspoon has a capacity of 5 millilitres.

Replacing 8 oz by 250 g and 8 fl oz by 250 ml, the table below provides a guide to convert weights and volume measures in recipes and also to indicate the appropriate metric weights where canned and packaged goods are used.

Although the yield is slightly greater (10%) the proportions remain the same.

Imperial ounces and fluid ounces		Metric grams and millilitres
½ oz	is replaced by	15 g
1 oz	"	30 g
2 oz	"	60 g
3 oz	"	90 g
4 oz (¼ lb)	"	125 g
5 oz	"	155 g
6 oz	"	185 g
7 oz	"	220 g
8 oz (½ lb)	"	250 g
9 oz	"	280 g
10 oz	"	315 g
11 oz	"	345 g
12 oz (¾ lb)	"	375 g
13 oz	"	410 g
14 oz	"	440 g
15 oz	"	470 g
16 oz (1 lb)	"	500 g (0.5 kg)
24 oz (1½ lb)	"	750 g
32 oz (2 lb)	"	1000 g (1 kg)
3 lb	"	1500 g (1.5 kg)
4 lb	"	2000 g (2 kg)

Figures in the table were obtained by multiplying the number of ounces or fluid ounces by the recommended metric equivalent 31.25 g (ml) = 1 oz (fl oz) and rounding the answer to the closest convenient number.

e.g. (5 fl oz) x (31.25 ml/fl oz) = 156.25 ml and rounded off is 155 ml.

OVEN TEMPERATURE

This is an approximate guide only. Different makes of stoves vary and even the same make of stove can give slightly different individual results at the same temperature. If in doubt with your particular stove, do refer to your own manufacturer's temperature chart. It is impossible in a general book to be exact for every stove, but the following is a good average guide in every case.

The following chart also gives approximate conversions from degrees Fahrenheit to degrees Celsius (formerly known as Centigrade). This chart can be used for conversion of recipes which give oven temperatures in metric measures.

Description of Oven	Thermostat Setting		
	$^\circ$F		$^\circ$C
	Automatic Electric	Gas	
Cool	200	200	90
Very slow	250	250	120
Slow	300-325	300	150-160
Moderately slow	325-350	325	160-170
Moderate	350-375	350	170-190
Moderately hot	375-400	375	190-200
Hot	400-450	400	200-230
Very hot	450-500	450	230-260

Abbreviations

Kilogram	kg
Gram	g
Millilitre	ml
Centimetre	cm
Millimetre	mm

ANTIPASTO AND SALADS

ANTIPASTO AND SALADS

Antipasti and Insalata

Antipasto simply means 'before meal' and Italians excel at serving interesting appetite provoking dishes before the meal. Most mid-day meals in Italy start with antipasto. Salami sausage, anchovies, olives, small artichokes in olive oil, pimientos in oil, mortadella sausage, fresh celery and fennel, raw green capsicum or their counterparts in pickles, sardines in olive oil, fresh cheeses such as ricotta are offered, either individually or together on a platter.

In the north there is a preference for more elaborate preparations like cold hard-boiled eggs in a variety of sauces, pickled artichokes or stuffed mushrooms.

In the south where vegetables grow in profusion — fresh fennel, capsicums and olives are served raw, or their pickled counterparts.

The beauty of antipasto, however, is that it may be as simple or elaborate as you wish, ranging from a few vegetables to a large assortment of meats and vegetables, almost like a Swedish smorgasbord.

The importance of a good olive oil in making antipasto cannot be overstressed. It is used to dress any vegetables, from raw celery or fennel, to cooked green beans or dried haricot beans. Just a little oil is sprinkled over the vegetables and a light squeeze of lemon juice, but it does wonders. When pepper is used, it is freshly ground from the pepper mill.

A word of explanation about Italian meals — antipasto is often dispensed with altogether. Sometimes a meal will start with soup or a pasta, but it is timely to mention that a rich thick minestrone **and** a pasta dish are never served at the same meal, nor is pasta served as a main dish in place of meat.

VINAIGRETTE DRESSING

Salso Vinaigrette

This is the traditional oil and vinegar dressing. Variations may be made by adding other ingredients. The classic proportions of a vinaigrette are three parts oil to one part vinegar, with salt and pepper to taste dissolved in the vinegar. Oil and vinegar can be mixed together or added to the salad separately. In Italy the oil and vinegar are brought to the table in their own containers, and one may dress the salad to one's own taste.

For a crisp salad, pour oil on first and toss well, insulating the leaves from vinegar and salt. Then add the vinegar. But if a slightly wilted salad is preferred — and many people do prefer it this way — first pour the vinegar and seasoning over. This method brings out the flavour of the leaves.

For some salads, cut down on the quantity of vinegar and use instead a squeeze of lemon juice, allowing the oil, which should be good quality, to predominate.

Flavoursome additions to this salad dressing are grated sharp cheese; chopped fresh herbs; mustard, either dry or prepared; and chopped hard-boiled egg.

ANTIPASTO MISTO

Mixed Antipasto

This makes a simple summer antipasto. On a long dish arrange an assortment of salads — raw capsicum cut into rings; raw mushrooms, sliced; potato salad; whole small red tomatoes, the plum shaped egg tomatoes are ideal; and fennel or celery, finely sliced. Sprinkle over a little Vinaigrette Dressing (see page 11) and top with hard-boiled eggs cut into quarters. Chopped parsley may be sprinkled over the top before serving.

MELON WITH PORT

Serves: 4

Ingredients	Metric	Imperial
Melons, rockmelon or honeydew	2 small	2 small
Port wine or marsala	250 ml	1 cup

Cut a triangle from each melon and remove seeds with a spoon. Fill melons with wine, replace triangles of melon and wrap in clear plastic wrap or place in plastic bags. Refrigerate for 2-3 hours, taking care that the wine does not spill out.

Cut melons in halves, reserving the wine, which is spooned back into the melon halves. Top with more wine if necessary. If small melons are not available, use a medium sized melon and cut into 4.

GREEN SALAD

The excellence of the oil in Italy can turn a simple dish into something very special — and it is especially important in the making of a good salad.

Green salad accompanies most meals in Italy, and while the choice of greens is dictated by the season, there is no limit to the variety available.

Use a combination of lettuce, escarole, curly endive, watercress, very young spinach. Even consider dandelion greens, but only the very young and tender leaves. In Italy these leaves are usually blanched by covering a young dandelion as it comes up in the garden with an upturned garden pot.

Add Vinaigrette Dressing (see page 11) at the last minute and toss until every leaf is glistening. Add salt and freshly ground pepper.

For an extra tang, freshly chopped herbs may be added or a little salt with a few anchovies, mashed with a little Vinaigrette Dressing, then put on top of the salad and tossed in with the ingredients.

RADISH AND GRUYERE SALAD

Insalata di Radicchio e Groviera
Serves: 4

Ingredients	Metric	Imperial
Crisp stale bread	1 slice	1 slice
Garlic	1 clove	1 clove
Sliced radishes	500 ml	2 cups
Gruyère cheese, cut in thin strips	60 g	2 oz
Vinaigrette Dressing (see page 11)	125 ml	½ cup

Rub slice of bread with cut clove of garlic, then break into fairly small pieces and put in a salad bowl. Add sliced radishes and strips of cheese, pour the Vinaigrette Dressing over evenly and toss well.

GREEii BEANS AND TUiiA

Serves: 4-6

Ingredients	Metric	Imperial
Green beans	500 g	1 lb
Olive oil	125 ml	½ cup
Lemon juice	1 teaspoon	1 teaspoon
Salt and freshly ground pepper	to season	to season
Tuna in oil	1 x 205 g can	1 x 6½ oz can

Top and tail beans, remove strings and leave whole. Cook in boiling salted water to cover until just tender, drain. While still hot, sprinkle with oil and lemon juice and season with salt and pepper. Drain tuna, break into large chunks and toss with beans. Cover and chill before serving.

NEAPOLITAN TOMATO SALAD

Insalata di Pomodori alla Napoletana
Serves: 6

Ingredients	Metric	Imperial
Tomatoes	6 large	6 large
Vinaigrette Dressing (see page 11)	125 ml	½ cup
Garlic	2 cloves	2 cloves
Chopped fresh basil	2 tablespoons	2 tablespoons

Peel and slice tomatoes. Arrange slices, overlapping, on a large salad platter and pour over the Vinaigrette Dressing into which the finely chopped garlic and basil have been mixed.

STEWED SWEET CAPSICUMS

Papriche Stufate

Capsicums appear in a mosaic of colours — red, green, yellow and orange. In Venice capsicums are served in a variety of ways, but they are never better than when cooked in the light Italian olive oil.

Serves: 4-6 as an antipasto

Ingredients	Metric	Imperial
Green or yellow capsicums	500 g	1 lb
Olive oil	125 ml	½ cup
Garlic	1 clove	1 clove
Tomatoes	500 g	1 lb
Salt and freshly ground pepper	to taste	to taste
Finely chopped parsley for garnish		

Wash capsicums, remove tops. Cut in halves, remove seeds and membrane. Cut flesh into strips. Heat oil in a saucepan and sauté clove of garlic gently until it begins to brown. Discard garlic. Add capsicum strips to pan and cook gently for 15 minutes. Peel and roughly chop tomatoes. Place tomatoes in a layer on top of capsicums, season to taste with salt and pepper and continue cooking gently until tomatoes are reduced to a thick sauce. Sprinkle with parsley.

Serve hot as a vegetable accompaniment to grilled steak or roast chicken, or serve cold, as a first course appetizer or part of an hors d'oeuvre platter.

STUFFED CAPSICUMS

Peperoni Ripieno

Use a combination of green and red capsicums to make an attractive platter.

Serves: 6 as an antipasto
Cooking time: 30 minutes
Oven temperature: 160-170°C (325-350°F)

Ingredients	Metric	Imperial
Even sized capsicums	6 small	6 small
Soft white breadcrumbs	375 ml	1½ cups
Tuna, flaked	1 x 185 g can	1 x 6 oz can
Black olives, coarsely chopped	125 ml	½ cup
Olive oil	125 ml	½ cup
Drained capers	2 tablespoons	2 tablespoons
Chopped parsley	2 tablespoons	2 tablespoons
Garlic, crushed	1 small clove	1 small clove
Salt and pepper	to taste	to taste
Stock	85 ml	1/3 cup

Slice tops off capsicums, remove seeds and membrane and parboil in simmering water about 5 minutes. Drain, cut side down on kitchen paper while preparing filling.

In a bowl, combine breadcrumbs with tuna, olives, olive oil, capers, parsley, garlic, salt and pepper. Stuff capsicums with mixture and pack them side by side in an ovenproof dish. Add stock. Bake in a moderately slow oven for about 30 minutes. Serve whole or slit in two lengthways, good either hot or cold as a first course.

PROSCIUTTO AND MELON (see page 23)

CROSTINI OF MOZZARELLA

This is a rich Neapolitan dish — sometimes made without the anchovy fillets. Crusty Italian bread may be used, although a neat sandwich loaf gives a better shape. The bread may also be cut with metal biscuit cutters in different shapes with the cheese cut similarly, this gives a very attractive appearance for more formal occasions.

Serves: 4

Ingredients	Metric	Imperial
Mozzarella cheese	250 g	8 oz
White bread	8 slices	8 slices
Anchovy fillets	8	8
Eggs, lightly beaten	2	2
Milk	125 ml	½ cup
Butter	15 g	½ oz
Olive oil	125 ml	½ cup

Place a thin slice of mozzarella cheese on 4 slices of bread. Cut anchovy fillets in 2 lengthways, and place on cheese. Cover with remaining bread. Trim off crusts and cut each sandwich in half. Dip sandwiches in combined beaten egg and milk and fry in hot butter and olive oil until golden brown on both sides. Fry a few at a time and use 2 forks to turn sandwiches over. Remove from pan and place on a piece of crumpled kitchen paper in a low oven to keep hot until all are cooked. Serve on a heated platter.

PORK IN TUNA MAYONNAISE

Maiale Tonnato
Serves: 8 as an antipasto, 4-6 as a main course

Ingredients	Metric	Imperial
Lean, boned loin of pork	1 kg	2 lb
Tuna in oil	185 ml	¾ cup
Onion, finely chopped	1	1
Anchovy fillets, chopped	8	8
Dry white wine	500 ml	2 cups
Salt and pepper	to season	to season
Olive oil	4 tablespoons	4 tablespoons
Lemon juice	2 tablespoons	2 tablespoons
Capers	1 teaspoon	1 teaspoon

Ask the butcher to bone the loin of pork, it should be stripped of fat. Place pork, tuna with oil from can, onion, anchovies, wine and salt and pepper in a heavy saucepan. Cover and cook gently over a low heat until meat is tender, about 2 hours. Place meat in a bowl or deep plate. Push ingredients in saucepan through a sieve or pulverise in an electric blender until smooth. Gradually work oil into mixture, a teaspoon at a time, as you do when making mayonnaise. Add lemon juice and capers.

Pour sauce over meat and let it stand overnight, covered. Serve sliced very thinly with the sauce. This will keep in refrigerator for a week.

Note: Pork fillets may be used for this dish, just reduce cooking time to 1½ hours. When serving, cut in slanting diagonal slices to get nice oval pieces.

BEAN SALADS

Serves: 6

Ingredients	Metric	Imperial
Dried baby lima beans	250 g	8 oz
Salt	to taste	to taste
Small onion	½	½
Chopped parsley	4 tablespoons	4 tablespoons
Garlic, crushed	1 clove	1 clove
Olive oil	3 tablespoons	3 tablespoons
White wine vinegar	2 tablespoons	2 tablespoons

Soak beans in cold water to cover for at least 6 hours. Drain, then place beans in a large saucepan and add enough cold water to cover. Bring to the boil, lower heat and simmer for 40-45 minutes, or until tender. Add salt to taste towards end of cooking time.

Drain beans and toss with thinly sliced onion, 1 tablespoon chopped parsley, garlic, oil and vinegar. Allow to cool. Sprinkle with remaining parsley before serving.

BEAN AND TUNA SALADS

Prepare Bean Salad (see above). Open 1 can good quality tuna in oil, separate tuna into large chunks and place on top of Bean Salad before serving.

SALAD OF FENNEL

Insalata di Finocchi
Serves: 4

Ingredients	Metric	Imperial
Fennel bulbs	2	2
Radishes	6	6
Cucumber	1	1
Hard-boiled eggs	2	2
Vinaigrette Dressing (see page 11)	125 ml	½ cup
Chopped mint	1 tablespoon	1 tablespoon

Slice fennel bulbs into thin strips. Finely slice radishes. Peel cucumber and cut into dice. Peel hard-boiled eggs and cut into quarters.

Arrange vegetables in a small dish. Season Vinaigrette Dressing with mint and sprinkle over vegetables. Garnish with eggs.

Note: This salad may be made with fennel only and the mint may be replaced with chopped parsley. Italian parsley with its strong flavour is best for Italian salads.

Variation: One orange, peeled and cut into segments, added to this salad makes it an excellent accompaniment to duck or poultry.

RAW MUSHROOM SALAD

Insalata di Funghi Crudi
Serves: 2

Ingredients	Metric	Imperial
Vinegar	2 tablespoons	2 tablespoons
Salt and pepper	to taste	to taste
Garlic	1 clove	1 clove
Olive oil	125 ml	½ cup
Sour cream (optional)	1 tablespoon	1 tablespoon
Button mushrooms	250 g	8 oz
Gruyère cheese	250 g	8 oz
Leg ham, thickly cut	250 g	8 oz

Mix vinegar, salt and pepper. Bruise garlic by striking with the flat of a knife and add to vinegar. Add oil and beat with a fork until combined. Remove garlic, stir in sour cream.

Wipe mushrooms with a damp cloth to remove any straw, trim stems and slice the caps thinly. Cut cheese and ham into julienne (matchstick size) strips. Add dressing to mushrooms, cheese and ham in a bowl and toss lightly. Pile into a serving dish. Serve as a first course.

POTATO SALAD

Insalata di Patate
Serves: 4

Ingredients	Metric	Imperial
Potatoes	500 g	1 lb
Garlic	1 clove	1 clove
Shallots, including green tops	6	6
Capers	1 tablespoon	1 tablespoon
Anchovy fillets (optional)	4	4
Vinaigrette Dressing (see page 11)	125 ml	½ cup
Mayonnaise (see page 50)	125 ml	½ cup

Scrub potatoes. Boil gently in their jackets for about 15-20 minutes or until tender. While still warm, peel and cut into dice. Crush garlic (this is optional and may be omitted), chop shallots and capers and add to potatoes. If anchovies are used, they may first be soaked in milk, this reduces the strong salty flavour, then chopped and added to potatoes. Pour the dressing over the potatoes while they are still warm. Toss lightly. Just before serving, fold in the Mayonnaise.

Variations: Capers and anchovies may be omitted, they would become monotonous if used too often. However, they add piquancy which is welcome in a potato salad. Mayonnaise is also optional, it adds a certain creaminess.

PROSCIUTTO AND MELON

Prosciutto con Mellone

Prosciutto is a raw ham cured in a special way. Parma ham, the classic for this dish, is not readily available, but a similar ham is now being made outside Italy. It is available at delicatessens and some Italian shops under various names, but perhaps prosciutto is the most common. It may take a little searching for but is well worth the effort. The ham should be cut in wafer thin slices.

Serves: 4

Ingredients	Metric	Imperial
Melons, rockmelon or honeydew	2 small	2 small
Prosciutto, thinly sliced	250 g	8 oz
Black pepper	to season	to season

Chill melons, cut each into 8 small wedges and remove seeds. The melon may be detached from the skin, if preferred. Serve with the very thinly sliced prosciutto, which is either arranged over the melon wedges, or rolled into neat cigarette shapes and served alongside. The only seasoning is coarsely ground black pepper, straight from the pepper mill.

Variation: When fresh figs are in season, serve them peeled with prosciutto on the side.

SOUPS

SOUPS

Minestra

Soups in Italy are many and varied. They range from delicate broths barely flavoured with a few thin slices of vegetable or a handful or pastina (soup pasta), to hearty, filling soups such as minestrone ('the big soup').

What gives most Italian soups their particular character is the lavish use of parmesan or pecorino cheese, which goes into the soup and also accompanies it separately at the table.

The Roman stracciatella is a light, easy to make soup. Egg beaten with salt, pepper, spices and parmesan cheese is poured into boiling broth, whipped for a second, then removed from the heat and served immediately. The egg cooks in light spicy flakes, making it an ideal dish to serve before a large or rich meal. It is also substantial enough for a quick snack, just add another egg.

At the other end of the scale is minestrone. Claims are made that it should be so thick with beans, vegetables and pasta that a soup spoon will stand up in it. Don't take this literally, but it is an indication that minestrone should indeed be a thick hearty dish.

BEEF BROTH

Brodo di Manso

Cooking time: 3 hours

Ingredients	Metric	Imperial
Shin of beef with bone	1 kg	2 lb
Carrots	2	2
Yellow turnip	1 small	1 small
Onion	1	1
Celery	1 stalk	1 stalk
Parsley	3 sprigs	3 sprigs
Tomato paste	1 teaspoon	1 teaspoon
Salt and pepper	to taste	to taste

Place meat and bone in a large saucepan, cover with water, about 5 litres (8 pints). Bring slowly to the boil, skim, then cover and simmer for 2 hours. Add vegetables cut into chunks, parsley sprigs and tomato paste, cover and simmer for a further 1 hour. Strain broth, season to taste and cool. Remove fat from the surface of the broth and use as a base for soups as required.

CHICKEN BROTH

Brodo Pollo

Cooking time: 3 hours

Ingredients	Metric	Imperial
Chicken necks, feet, backs	1 kg	2 lb
Celery	1 stalk	1 stalk
Carrots	2	2
Onion	1	1
Parsley	3 sprigs	3 sprigs
Tomato paste	2 teaspoons	2 teaspoons
Salt and pepper	to taste	to taste

Place chicken pieces in a large saucepan, cover with water, about 2.5 litres (4 pints). Bring slowly to boiling point, skim and simmer for 2 hours. Add vegetables cut into chunks, parsley sprigs and tomato paste, cover and simmer for 1 hour more. Strain and cool. Before using, remove any fat from the surface. Use as a base for soups.

VEGETABLE SOUP FRIULI STYLE

Iota Friulana
Serves: 6

Ingredients	Metric	Imperial
Dried haricot beans	250 g	8 oz
White cabbage	½ head	½ head
Celery	1 bunch	1 bunch
Garlic	1 clove	1 clove
Fat bacon or speck	60 g	2 oz
Parsley	2-3 sprigs	2-3 sprigs
Onion	1	1
Sage leaves	2	2
Salt and pepper	to taste	to taste
Grated parmesan cheese for serving		

Soak beans in cold water overnight. Drain, put into a large pan and cover with fresh cold water. Cook without salt until tender, about 1½ hours. Drain beans, reserve liquid and add boiling water to make liquid up to 2 litres (8 cups). Return beans and liquid to pan.

Wash cabbage and shred finely. Chop celery. On a wooden board chop garlic, bacon, parsley, onion and sage together as finely as possible. Add all these ingredients to soup with salt and pepper. Cover pan and simmer 1 hour. Serve hot, sprinkled with grated parmesan cheese.

BROTH WITH EGG FLAKES

Brodo con Tagliarini

Egg flakes are tiny pasta squares sometimes sold as tagliarini.
Other small varieties of pasta may be used in place of
tagliarini, the soup then takes the name of the pasta — alphabet,
tripolini (small egg bows), acini di pepe (peppercorns) etc.

Serves: 4

Ingredients	Metric	Imperial
Chicken Broth (see page 26)	1 litre	4 cups
Egg flakes	2 tablespoons	2 tablespoons
Chopped parsley	2 teaspoons	2 teaspoons

Bring chicken broth to the boil, add pasta and cook 4-5 minutes,
or until pasta is tender. Add parsley and serve.

EGG DROP SOUP

Stracciatella
Serves: 4

Ingredients	Metric	Imperial
Chicken Broth (see page 26)	1 litre	4 cups
Eggs	2 large	2 large
Grated parmesan cheese	2 tablespoons	2 tablespoons
Nutmeg	pinch	pinch

Bring chicken broth to the boil. Whip eggs to a froth, add
cheese and nutmeg. Add egg mixture to boiling broth, whip for
a second or two with a fork, then remove from heat. Serve as
quickly as possible.

Note: The egg mixture will not be smooth, it just breaks into flakes.

LEMON EGG DROP SOUP

Make soup as above, but add 2 tablespoons lemon juice to egg mixture while whipping the eggs, then proceed with recipe.

MUSHROOM SOUP

Zuppa di Funghi
Serves: 6

Ingredients	Metric	Imperial
Bacon rashers	2	2
Butter	60 g	2 oz
Chopped parsley	1 tablespoon	1 tablespoon
Mushrooms	500 g	1 lb
Chicken or Beef Broth (see page 26)	1.5 litres	6 cups
Salt and pepper	to taste	to taste
Egg	1	1
Grated parmesan cheese	60 ml	¼ cup

Finely chop bacon rashers and cook gently in butter until bacon fat is clear and becoming crisp on the edges. Add parsley and thinly sliced mushrooms and cook over a slow heat for 5 minutes. Bring broth to the boil in another saucepan, add mushrooms, season to taste and simmer covered for 15 minutes.

Beat egg with cheese, add a little hot soup and blend together. Stir into the soup.

SOUP PAVESE STYLE

Zuppa alla Pavese

This originated in 1525. Francis 1, King of France, was losing the battle of Pavia. He stopped at a small farm cottage and asked for a meal. The farmer's wife was about to serve a simple soup, but with the proper sense of the occasion, she enriched the soup with toasted bread, an egg and some parmesan cheese. The monarch ate the soup, thanked the peasants and declared, 'what you have given me was a king's soup'. It became known as Zuppa alla Pavese.

Serves: 6

Ingredients	Metric	Imperial
Butter	125 g	4 oz
Italian bread	6 thick slices	6 thick slices
Eggs	6	6
Salt	¼ teaspoon	¼ teaspoon
Grated parmesan cheese	125 ml	½ cup
Chicken Broth (see page 26)	1.5 litres	6 cups

Melt butter in a frying pan and sauté bread until golden, but still soft in the centre. Place bread slices in warmed soup bowls. (If Italian bread is not available, use crusty French bread or Vienna loaf). Carefully break an egg into each bowl. Sprinkle each egg with a little salt and grated cheese.

Boil broth and very carefully ladle a cup of boiling broth into each bowl. Keep broth over heat while working so that it remains hot enough to poach the eggs in the bowls. Add broth carefully to the bowls in order not to break the eggs. Serve immediately.

Note: It is possible to poach eggs beforehand and add to the broth in the bowls. This does cause the subtle flavour of the soup to change. Eggs will be cooked sufficiently for most people if the broth is really boiling when ladled into the bowls.

MINESTRONE MILANESE

Serves: 6-8

Ingredients	Metric	Imperial
Dried haricot beans	250 g	8 oz
Pickled pork, diced	250 g	8 oz
Onion, chopped	1	1
Carrot, diced	1 large	1 large
Diced celery	125 ml	½ cup
Cabbage, shredded	½ small head	½ small head
Beef Broth (see page 26)	3.75 litres	6 pints
Potatoes, diced	2 medium sized	2 medium sized
Rice	125 ml	½ cup
Chopped parsley	1 tablespoon	1 tablespoon
Garlic, finely chopped	1 clove	1 clove
Basil leaves, chopped	2	2
Thyme, chopped	1 sprig	1 sprig
Grated parmesan cheese for serving		

Soak haricot beans overnight, drain and place in a saucepan. Cover with water and cook gently for 1 hour. Check water to make sure it doesn't boil away.

Sauté pickled pork with onion until onion is soft. Do not allow onion to brown. If saucepan is not a heavy one, it may be necessary to add a tablespoon of butter. Add carrot, celery, cabbage and drained, partly cooked beans. Cover and cook gently for 15 minutes, stirring occasionally. Add broth and potatoes and cook slowly for a further 1½ hours. If soup becomes too thick, add a little water.

Add rice and cook for 10 minutes over a high heat. Add parsley, garlic, basil and thyme. Serve with a bowl of parmesan cheese.

PASTA

RADISH AND GRUYERE SALAD (see page 13)

PASTA

There are many theories about the origins of pasta. It is said that Marco Polo returned to Italy from the Orient with the formula. A food called makari ('blessed things') is described in eighth century Greek writings as a dish made of dough and served with a sauce. The Neapolitans have their own legend of a cardinal from their city exclaiming 'Ma cari! Ma caroni' (Why the dears! Why the big dears) when presented with a new dish, it was made with dough and served with a sauce.

Whatever, Italy has adopted pasta as her own.

It is made in countless different shapes, the catalogue of one big firm lists over fifty varieties. Some varieties are meant to be eaten merely with a sauce, others are filled with meat, chopped spinach, cheese and other ingredients. Ravioli is perhaps the best known of these.

More important than the size or shape of pasta is the sauce. It may be a simple sauce of melted butter, or butter with mashed anchovies and garlic, or beautiful pesto, the green sauce from Genoa, made by mixing chopped basil, pine nuts, oil and parmesan cheese, or the rich meat ragu known to the world as bolognese.

There are two main distinctions to be made with regard to Italian pasta. One is *pasta fatta in casa* (home-made pasta) and the kind that is mass produced and sold dried in packets. There is much to be said for both, but if you have a light hand with pastry, it is well worth making your own pasta.

HOW TO COOK PASTA

Use a large pan with plenty of room for pasta to cook, without sticking. Allow 3.75 litres (6 pints) water for 250 g (8 oz) pasta. Add about 1 teaspoon salt for each litre of water and have the water boiling vigorously before adding pasta. A teaspoon of olive oil may be added to water to help prevent pasta sticking together, a good tip, especially for large pasta like lasagne.

Drop pasta into water slowly so water does not go off the boil. Stir a few times at start of cooking to prevent pasta sticking, then allow to boil vigorously. When cooked, pasta must be tender but still firm 'al dente', as the Italians say — which means just firm enough to bite comfortably, not so soft that it is mushy. When cooked, remove immediately from heat and drain. Pour boiling water through pasta, then allow to drain.

Home-made pasta will not take as long to cook as the bought variety, but it is difficult to give exact times as this depends on the thickness of the dough and also the shape. There is a guide to cooking times with each recipe, but the best way is to start tasting and testing pasta once it rises to the surface of the water. When cooked, drain, toss in sauce or butter and serve immediately.

Approximate cooking times for bought packaged pasta:
Spaghetti: 12 minutes.
Tagliatelle (long ribbon strips): 8 minutes.
Vermicelli (long thin threads): 8-10 minutes.
Canneloni (large pipes or squares): 12 minutes.

Servings: 500 g (1 lb) pasta will serve 4 people as a main course, 6 people as a first course.

TO COMBINE PASTA AND SAUCE

Place drained cooked pasta in a warm serving bowl, add part of the sauce (if desired, sprinkled with grated parmesan cheese). With 2 forks, or spaghetti tongs, toss gently until pasta is coated with sauce. Top with remaining sauce.

TO KEEP PASTA HOT

For a short while, you may return drained cooked pasta to the empty cooking pan, add about 60 g (2 oz) butter, then cover with a lid and keep warm.

For best results, serve pasta immediately, but if this is inconvenient, drain in a colander and set over a pan containing a small amount of simmering water. Coat pasta with 90 g (3 oz) butter (for 6 servings) to keep it from sticking together. Cover colander.

EGG PASTA

Pasta Gialla
Serves: 4

Ingredients	Metric	Imperial
Plain flour	500 ml	2 cups
Eggs	2	2
Cold water	to mix	to mix

Sift flour into a bowl, making a well in the centre and add eggs. Stir with a knife, adding a little cold water (about 3 tablespoons) and form into a firm dough with hands. Turn out on to a floured board and knead, turning and pushing with the heel of your hand for about 15 minutes, or until dough is smooth and pliable. The dough will be stiff at first but will become more pliable as you knead. Shape into a ball and wrap in clear plastic wrap. Leave to rest for 20 minutes.

Roll dough out to a paper thin even sheet on a lightly floured surface. Sprinkle lightly with flour to prevent sticking. Cut into required shapes (see pages 37 40 41) and cook in a large saucepan of boiling salted water. Dough can be left for 30 minutes before cooking, but sprinkle liberally with plain flour to prevent it sticking. Use in any of the following recipes.

Note: This quantity of dough can be doubled, but divide it in half before rolling out.

PASTA WITH BUTTER

Pasta al Burro
Serves: 4

Cook 500 g (1 lb) pasta, home-made or bought ribbon noodles, spaghetti or macaroni, in usual way until tender. Drain, turn into a warm serving bowl and top generously with butter and grated parmesan cheese. Stir through pasta until coated. Serve extra butter and cheese at the table.

RIBBON NOODLES ALFREDO

Tagliatelle Alfredo
Serves: 4

Cook 500 g (1 lb) home-made or bought ribbon noodles until 'al dente'. Drain well in a colander. Melt 60 g (2 oz) butter in same saucepan over a low heat. Mix in 250 ml (1 cup) cream, then toss in noodles, 250 ml (1 cup) grated parmesan cheese and a good grind of black pepper. Toss well and serve immediately.

NOODLES WITH PESTO

Pasta col Pesto
Serves: 4

Cook 500 g (1 lb) home-made or bought fine ribbon noodles until 'al dente'. Drain and pile into a warm serving bowl. Heap Pesto alla Genovese (see page 52) on top with 60 g (2 oz) butter and serve. Mix pesto into pasta at the table. Serve with a separate bowl of grated pecorini or parmesan cheese.

SPAGHETTI BOLOGNESE

Serves: 4

Cook 500 g (1 lb) spaghetti until 'al dente'. Drain and turn into a warm serving bowl, add half the Bolognese Sauce (see page 48) and toss with 2 forks until each strand is evenly coated. Top with remaining sauce and sprinkle with grated parmesan cheese. Serve immediately.

RAVIOLI

Serves: 4

Prepare Egg Pasta (see page 35), using only 375 ml (1½ cups) flour and less water, about 1 tablespoon. This dough should be softer than for other pasta.

Halve kneaded dough. Roll each portion out thinly on a floured board to a long oblong shape. Cover first piece with damp kitchen paper to prevent drying out. Place teaspoonfuls of filling (see page 38) in mounds at 5 cm (2-inch) intervals in regular lines on second sheet of pasta. Brush between mounds of filling with water, then place reserved sheet of dough over top. Press **firmly** between mounds, sealing the two sheets of dough together, then, using a pastry wheel, cut into squares.

Drop Ravioli into a large pan of boiling salted water and cook 15 minutes or until tender (cooking time depends on thinness of dough). Drain and toss in melted butter and grated parmesan cheese, or in Bolognese Sauce (see page 48). Serve immediately.

Note: Meat filled Ravioli is often served in Chicken Broth (see page 26) as a soup.

Dough for Ravioli can also be cut into 35 mm (1½-inch) rounds, then filled and the dough folded over to make half moons. Press edges well together and mark with a fork.

MEAT FILLING FOR RAVIOLI

Ingredients	Metric	Imperial
Garlic	1 small clove	1 small clove
Butter	30 g	1 oz
Minced steak	250 g	8 oz
Finely chopped parsley	1 tablespoon	1 tablespoon
Soft breadcrumbs	3 tablespoons	3 tablespoons
Grated parmesan cheese	2 tablespoons	2 tablespoons
Freshly grated nutmeg	good pinch	good pinch
Salt and pepper	to taste	to taste
Egg	1	1

Chop garlic. Heat butter in pan and fry meat, stirring, until beginning to brown. Add garlic and parsley and continue cooking, stirring with a fork, until meat is well browned. Place in a bowl and add breadcrumbs, cheese, grated nutmeg and salt and pepper to taste. Mix all together, then stir in beaten egg. Combine thoroughly. Makes enough filling for one quantity of pasta.

GREEN PASTA

Pasta Verde
Serves: 6-8

Ingredients	Metric	Imperial
Frozen chopped spinach	1 x 315 g pkt	1 x 10 oz pkt
Plain flour	625 ml	2½ cups
Egg	1	1
Cold water or extra plain flour	to mix	to mix

Put spinach in a saucepan and stir over a low heat until melted. Turn into a fine sieve and press with a spoon to extract all liquid. When cool enough to handle, squeeze spinach with hand to extract as much remaining liquid as possible.

Sift flour into a bowl, make well in centre. Put egg and spinach in well and stir with a knife, gradually incorporating flour. It may be necessary to add a little cold water — or more flour — to make a firm dough. Knead on a floured board until smooth, about 15 minutes. Wrap in clear plastic wrap and leave to rest for 20 minutes.

Halve dough. Roll out on a floured board until very thin. Cut into required shapes as for Egg Pasta (see page 35) and use in recipes instead of Egg Pasta. One of the best ways is simple — with butter and cheese (see Pasta al Burro, page 38).

RIBBON NOODLES

Tagliatelle

Roll pasta dough to an oblong shape. Starting from the shorter side, roll up dough, then cut across roll into 10 mm (½-inch) strips. Unravel each strip and drop into boiling salted water for about 5 minutes or until pasta is tender. Drain and serve with a sauce or with butter and grated parmesan cheese.

TAGLIOLINI

Roll up dough as above but cut in thin 5 mm (¼-inch) strips. Serve similarly or in soup.

LASAGNE

Cut rolled out pasta in oblongs about 8 x 10 cm (3 x 4-inches). Place on a floured baking tray so they are not touching. Bring large pan of salted water to the boil and drop in pasta. Cook about 10 minutes or until tender, then drain and rinse. Spread on a clean cloth, again not touching. Use in Baked Green Lasagne (see page 41). Lasagne can be left 2 hours before cooking. As it is larger than other pasta, it is best cooked in 2-3 lots, more if your pan is small.

This dough can be made into other shapes such as bows, if liked.

BAKED GREEN LASAGNE

Lasagne Verde al Forno
Serves: 6-8
Cooking time: 1 hour
Oven temperature: 170-190ºC (350-375ºF)

Ingredients	Metric	Imperial
Green Pasta (see page 47) or packaged green lasagne	1 quantity 500 g	1 quantity 1 lb
Bolognese Sauce (see page 47)	1 quantity	1 quantity
Béchamel Sauce (see page 47)	double quantity	double quantity
Grated nutmeg	pinch	pinch
Grated parmesan cheese	125 ml	½ cup

If making fresh Green Pasta (see page 47) prepare dough, divide
in half and roll each half out thinly to a rectangle, 40 x 45 cm
(16 x 18-inches). Trim edges and cut dough into oblongs
8 x 10 cm (3 x 4-inches). Add salt to a large pan of rapidly
boiling water and drop in pasta oblongs one at a time. Cook in
at least 2 lots. Boil pasta until tender, about 10 minutes for
home-made pasta, 15 minutes for bought. Turn into colander,
rinse with cold water and place pasta on a clean cloth so they
are not touching.

Prepare Bolognese Sauce and double quantity of Béchamel
Sauce, flavouring it with freshly grated nutmeg.

Put a layer of Bolognese Sauce in the base of a large deep
ovenproof dish. Top with some Béchamel Sauce, then a layer
of pasta. Repeat until dish is full, ending with Bolognese, then
Béchamel Sauce. Sprinkle with parmesan cheese and bake in a
moderate oven for 1 hour.

Note: This dish can also be made using Egg Pasta (see page 35).
A richer dish can be made by including slices of mozzarella
cheese after each layer of Béchamel Sauce. Sometimes a beaten
egg is added to the last layer of Béchamel Sauce for a custard-
like topping.

LASAGNE WITH RICOTTA CHEESE

Lasagne con la Ricotta

This casserole of lasagne noodles, ricotta cheese with flavourings and bolognese sauce can be made with fresh, home-made noodles (see page 47) or with packaged bought lasagne noodles. If ricotta cheese is not available, use a creamy cottage cheese.

Serves: 6
Cooking time: 45 minutes
Oven temperature: 170-190°C (350-375°F)

Ingredients	Metric	Imperial
Bolognese Sauce (see page 48)	1 quantity	1 quantity
Lasagne noodles	375 g	12 oz
Ricotta cheese	500 g	1 lb
Grated parmesan cheese	125 ml	½ cup
Chopped parsley	1 tablespoon	1 tablespoon
Eggs	2	2
Salt	2 teaspoons	2 teaspoons
Ground pepper	½ teaspoon	½ teaspoon
Mozzarella cheese	500 g	1 lb

Prepare Bolognese Sauce. Cook lasagne in a large pan of boiling water until tender, about 15 minutes. Drain and rinse with cold water. Combine ricotta cheese with parmesan cheese, parsley, slightly beaten eggs, salt and pepper.

Grease a large oval baking dish, approximately 35 x 23 x 5 cm (14 x 9 x 2-inches). Place a layer of noodles in the base. Cover them with half the cheese filling, spread filling with half the mozarella cheese, thinly sliced and cover with half the Bolognese Sauce. Repeat layers. Bake in a moderate oven for 45 minutes. Stand for 10 minutes to allow filling to set slightly, then cut into squares to serve.

PASTA SHELLS WITH CAPSICUMS

Conchiglie alla Peperonata

A mixture of yellow, green and red capsicums makes this a colourful dish, though green capsicums alone may be used.

Serves: 4-6

Ingredients	Metric	Imperial
Capsicums	4 small	4 small
Tomatoes	500 g	1 lb
Onion	1	1
Olive oil	2 tablespoons	2 tablespoons
Butter	30 g	1 oz
Chopped fresh basil	2-3 tablespoons	2-3 tablespoons
Salt and pepper	to taste	to taste
Pasta shells	500 g	1 lb
Grated parmesan cheese for serving		

Halve capsicums, remove seeds and membrane and cut into strips. Drop tomatoes into boiling water for 20 seconds, then plunge into cold water. Slip skins off tomatoes, then quarter and remove seeds. Cut tomato flesh in dice. Thinly slice onion.

Heat oil and butter and cook onion gently until just coloured. Add capsicum strips and cook over a high heat, stirring, until beginning to soften. Add tomatoes, basil and salt and pepper to taste. Cover and cook gently for 15 minutes. Remove lid and continue cooking until water evaporates. Adjust seasoning.

Cook pasta shells in plenty of boiling salted water until tender. Drain well. Turn into a warm serving dish and top with capsicum mixture. Toss lightly to mix and sprinkle generously with cheese. Serve immediately.

MACARONI WITH HAM AND EGGS

Macheroni alla Carbonara

Any shaped macaroni or spaghetti can be used for this Roman dish. The simple sauce of ham and eggs is a pleasant change from the more usual tomato or spicy sauces.

Serves: 4

Ingredients	Metric	Imperial
Macaroni	500 g	1 lb
Ham or bacon	125 g	4 oz
Butter	90 g	3 oz
Eggs	2	2
Grated parmesan cheese for serving		

Cook macaroni in a large pan of boiling salted water for about 15 minutes or until tender but still firm. Drain and turn into a heated serving dish.

While macaroni cooks, cut ham into julienne (matchstick size) strips and cook gently in a small pan in a little butter for about 5 minutes. Beat eggs slightly. Just before serving, stir eggs into fried ham and cook over a low heat, stirring until eggs just start to thicken. Before they turn into scrambled eggs, toss with macaroni and the remaining butter. Top with grated parmesan cheese and serve with more parmesan separately.

Note: There is another way to make this dish. Cook pasta, drain, add cooked ham or bacon and while pasta is still very hot, add beaten eggs and stir. The heat of the pasta is sufficient to cook the eggs.

SAUCES

SAUCES

Salse

Sauces are important to Italian cooking and although along with the French and English, Italians are enthusiastic about mayonnaise and bechamel sauce, they have developed their own robust sauces that go so well with Italian food.

Tomato sauce, pesto, and bolognese sauce are perhaps the most famous. They are simple to prepare and cook, and have a certain 'freshness' about them.

The pomadori, or apple of gold as the tomato is often called, sets the stage for many Italian dishes and tomato sauce is the basis of many regional specialities. Ingredients are added to it as suits local tastes; prosciutto from Bologna, onion and bacon of the Roman countryside, the clams of Naples, and local fresh cheeses and fish.

Flavourings may change and the length of time a sauce is cooked may change, but this only determines the characteristics of the sauce as it changes from province to province.

BÉCHAMEL SAUCE

Besciamella

This classic white sauce is for vegetables, boiled meats —
especially corned beef — and poached chicken. It also forms
the basis of many other sauces and features in many pasta
dishes.

Makes: 2 cups

Ingredients	Metric	Imperial
Milk	625 ml	1 pint
Bay leaf	1	1
Onion or	½	½
shallot	1	1
Whole peppercorns	5	5
Butter	60 g	2 oz
Plain flour	4 tablespoons	4 tablespoons
Cream (optional)	4 tablespoons	4 tablespoons
Freshly grated nutmeg	pinch	pinch
Salt and white pepper	to taste	to taste

Put milk, bay leaf, onion and peppercorns in a saucepan. Place
over a moderate heat until bubbles form around sides of pan.
Remove from heat and stand 5 minutes to infuse. Strain.

Melt butter in a small heavy saucepan, draw away from heat and
stir in flour. Return to a low heat and cook for 2 minutes,
stirring. Add strained milk all at once and stir constantly with a
wooden spoon or wire whisk, until sauce boils and thickens.
Add cream, nutmeg, salt and pepper to taste.

Note: If sauce is prepared in advance, cover surface with a
piece of damp greaseproof paper to prevent a skin forming.

BOLOGNESE SAUCE

Ragù alla Bolognese

Ragù is the sauce from Bologna that people all over the world love to serve with spaghetti. The true ragu is not just a sauce of tomato-flavoured minced meat, its ingredients include several kinds of meat, chicken livers and good uncured bacon or better still prosciutto. Sometimes a small cup of cream is added to the sauce just before it is tossed with the hot pasta, also try including a good piece of butter. Bolognese cooks claim the cream or the butter makes a smoother sauce.

Makes: Sauce for 500 g (1 lb) pasta

Ingredients	Metric	Imperial
Lean steak, finely chopped	250 g	8 oz
Lean pork, finely chopped	250 g	8 oz
Bacon or prosciutto, chopped	60 g	2 oz
Olive oil	1 tablespoon	1 tablespoon
Garlic, peeled	1 clove	1 clove
Onion, finely chopped	1 small	1 small
Chopped parsley	1 tablespoon	1 tablespoon
Bay leaf	1	1
Whole peeled tomatoes	1 x 500 g can	1 x 16 oz can
White wine	125 ml	½ cup
Water	125 ml	½ cup
Tomato paste	2 tablespoons	2 tablespoons
Salt and pepper	to season	to season
Chopped fresh basil	pinch	pinch
Butter or cream (optional)		

Put chopped steak, pork and bacon, mixed well together, into a saucepan with oil, garlic, onion, parsley, and bay leaf, and brown slowly, stirring frequently to prevent meat cooking in lumps. As soon as garlic turns golden, remove it and discard.

Add tomatoes (with juice from can), wine, water, tomato paste, salt and pepper. Cover and simmer for 1 hour. Add basil, cook

1 minute longer. Remove from heat and add a little butter or a few spoonfuls of cream.

Variation: If liked, substitute 250 g (8 oz) chicken livers for pork and add an extra 60 g (2 oz) bacon.

TOMATO SAUCE

Salsa di Pomodori

For pasta, meat and fish.

Makes: 1½ cups or enough for 500 g (1 lb) pasta

Ingredients	Metric	Imperial
Olive oil	2 tablespoons	2 tablespoons
Onion, finely chopped	1 small	1 small
Tomatoes, skinned, seeded and chopped or	1 kg	2 lb
whole peeled tomatoes	2 x 875 g cans	2 x 1 lb 12 oz can
Salt	½ teaspoon	½ teaspoon
Sugar	½ teaspoon or to taste	½ teaspoon or to taste
Pepper	¼ teaspoon	¼ teaspoon
Basil	2 leaves	2 leaves
or oregano	1 sprig	1 sprig
Bay leaf	1	1
Tomato paste	1 tablespoon	1 tablespoon

Heat oil, add onion and cook over a high heat for 5-6 minutes, stirring until brown. Add tomatoes (if using canned tomatoes, drain first, then chop), salt, sugar, pepper, basil, bay leaf and tomato paste. Return to heat and bring to the boil. Lower heat, cover and simmer for 45 minutes, stirring occasionally.

Sauce may be pushed through a sieve to make a smooth purée if desired.

Note: Tomato Sauce may be cooked for 15 minutes only, this gives a fresher tomato taste, which is preferred by some.

MAYONNAISE

Maionese

Italian Mayonnaise is made with egg yolks and olive oil only, and sometimes a little lemon juice. The result is perfectly delicious, perhaps it is the excellent oil that is used, also Italian cooks often start with an extra egg yolk.

Makes: 1 cup

Ingredients	Metric	Imperial
Egg yolks	2	2
Salt	½ teaspoon	½ teaspoon
White pepper	pinch	pinch
Lemon juice	2 teaspoons	2 teaspoons
Olive oil, best quality	250 ml	1 cup

Mayonnaise is easiest to make when ingredients are at room temperature. If eggs have been taken straight from the refrigerator, warm the bowl first to take the chill off the yolks.

Put egg yolks, salt, pepper and 1 teaspoon lemon juice into a bowl. Wrap a damp cloth around base of bowl to keep it firmly in place. Beat vigorously with a wire whisk and when egg yolks are thick, start adding oil, drop by drop from the tines of a fork, until a little more than 60 ml (¼ cup) has been added. As mixture thickens, add remaining oil in a thin stream, beating constantly. Stop now and then to check that mixture is blending well. If mixture becomes too thick, beat in a few drops of lemon juice to thin, then continue adding oil. When all the oil has been added, stir in remaining lemon juice. Check seasoning and blend in more salt and pepper if liked, to taste. Two teaspoons boiling water may be beaten into prepared Mayonnaise as a precaution against curdling. Cover and store at room temperature.
Variations: Green Mayonnaise (Maionese Verde): To Mayonnaise, add a good handful of parsley or fresh basil, very finely chopped.

Tuna Mayonnaise (Maionese Tonnata): To 250 ml (1 cup) Mayonnaise, add 85 ml (1/3 cup) canned tuna which has been pounded or pulverised in a blender. Serve with hard-boiled eggs or cold chicken or veal. Excellent in sandwiches or for filling small tomatoes for antipasto.

WHITE SAUCE FOR PASTA

Makes: enough for 250 g (8 oz) pasta

Ingredients	Metric	Imperial
Smoked bacon or ham	250 g	8 oz
Garlic	1 clove	1 clove
Coarsely ground pepper	½ teaspoon	½ teaspoon
Grated cheese	60 ml	¼ cup

Chop bacon into small pieces, finely chop garlic. Fry bacon, garlic and pepper together until bacon is crisp. (If using ham, cook lightly.) Spoon over pasta and sprinkle with grated cheese.

GREEN SAUCE

Salsa Verde

For dressing raw or cooked vegetables for antipasto, also cold cooked brains or sweetbreads. Good also with fish and cold meats.

Makes: ¾ cup

Ingredients	Metric	Imperial
Olive oil	125 ml	½ cup
Lemon juice	1 tablespoon	1 tablespoon
Chopped parsley	4 tablespoons	4 tablespoons
Chopped capers	1 tablespoon	1 tablespoon
Garlic, finely chopped	1-2 cloves	1-2 cloves
Anchovy fillets, chopped	1-2	1-2

Beat all ingredients together with a fork, until well blended. The sauce should be rather thick. The anchovy is optional.

GARLIC AND OIL SAUCE

Makes: enough for 500 g (1 lb) pasta

Ingredients	Metric	Imperial
Garlic, finely chopped	4-6 cloves	4-6 cloves
Olive oil	125 ml	½ cup
Salt and pepper	to taste	to taste

Cook garlic gently in oil. Drain pasta well and pour garlic and oil over. Stir thoroughly, season with salt and pepper and serve at once.

GREEN SAUCE GENOVESE

Pesto alla Genovese

This is the famous sauce which is eaten by the Genoese with all kinds of pasta and gnocchi. It is also added to soups — try a tablespoon stirred into minestrone or a chicken broth at the last minute, or a spoonful with baked jacket potatoes.

Makes: enough for 750 g (1½ lb) pasta

Ingredients	Metric	Imperial
Garlic, chopped	2-3 cloves	2-3 cloves
Finely chopped fresh basil	4-6 tablespoons	4-6 tablespoons
Chopped parsley	4 tablespoons	4 tablespoons
Pine nuts or walnuts	1 tablespoon	1 tablespoon
Grated parmesan or romano cheese	125 ml	½ cup
Olive oil	about 250 ml	about 1 cup
Freshly ground pepper	to season	to season

With a mortar and pestle, pound garlic, basil, parsley, pine nuts and cheese together until smooth. Gradually add oil, whisking between additions. Add enough oil, whisking all the time, until sauce is thick and smooth. Season with pepper.

Note: If made in large quantities, sauce can be made in a blender. Store in a jar in refrigerator, covered with a layer of olive oil.

EGG
DISHES

EGG DISHES

Egg dishes are popular in Italy, they are served mainly for lunch or supper, but are never part of an Italian breakfast.

Frittata, the Italian omelette is firm and usually well cooked. It is browned on both sides and served flat, cut into two or four. It often includes chopped vegetables, fish or meat and is an excellent way of using up leftovers.

Eggs are often served in the small ramekins or ovenproof dishes in which they are cooked.

ITALIAN STYLE FRIED EGGS

Uova Fritte all'Italiana
Serves: 4
Cooking time: 5 minutes
Oven temperature: 200-230°C (400-450°F)

Ingredients	Metric	Imperial
Olive oil	2 tablespoons	2 tablespoons
Eggs	4	4
Salt and pepper	to season	to season
Grated parmesan cheese	2 teaspoons	2 teaspoons

Heat oil in a frying pan, then break in eggs. Fry over a gentle heat until eggs are almost set, then sprinkle with salt and pepper. Remove pan from heat and sprinkle grated cheese over eggs, then place pan in a hot oven for 5 minutes, or until cheese melts.

Note: If your frying pan doesn't have an ovenproof handle, hold pan under a hot grill for a few seconds to melt the cheese.

PROSCIUTTO SOUFFLÉ

Soufflé di Prosciutto
Serves: 4
Cooking time: 30 minutes
Oven temperature: 190-200ºC (375-400ºF)

Ingredients	Metric	Imperial
Soft white breadcrumbs	2 tablespoons	2 tablespoons
Butter	90 g	3 oz
Grated parmesan cheese	1 tablespoon	1 tablespoon
Milk	440 ml	1¾ cups
Bay leaf	½	½
Prosciutto or ham	125 g	4 oz
Plain flour	3 tablespoons	3 tablespoons
Egg yolks	3	3
Cream	2 tablespoons	2 tablespoons
Grated nutmeg	pinch	pinch
Salt and pepper	to taste	to taste
Egg whites	4	4

Butter the inside of a 1.25 litre (2-pint) soufflé dish and sprinkle with 1 tablespoon breadcrumbs. Tie a double band of greaseproof paper around dish so it stands 5 cm (2-inches) above top of soufflé dish.

Melt 15 g (½ oz) butter in pan and fry remaining breadcrumbs, stirring constantly, until golden. Drain on absorbent paper, allow to cool. Mix with grated cheese and set aside.

Pour milk into saucepan, add bay leaf, cover and place over a very low heat to infuse for about 7 minutes. Do not boil. Remove bay leaf and cool milk slightly. Chop prosciutto finely. Melt remaining butter in a heavy saucepan, add flour and cook over a low heat, stirring, for 2 minutes. Remove from heat and add milk all at once. Cook, stirring constantly until sauce boils and thickens, then lower heat and continue to cook, stirring, for 2-3 minutes. Remove from heat and beat in egg yolks, one at a time. Add cream, nutmeg and prosciutto. Season with salt and pepper to taste.

Whip egg whites until stiff and fold gently but quickly into prosciutto mixture. Turn into prepared soufflé dish and sprinkle top of soufflé with breadcrumb and cheese mixture. Run a knife around top of soufflé, about 2.5 cm (1-inch) from edge of dish to form a crown when soufflé bakes. Cook in a moderately hot oven for 30 minutes. Serve immediately.

EGGS IN ANCHOVY BUTTER

Uova al Forna con Acciuga
Serves: 4
Cooking time: 8-10 minutes
Oven temperature: 200-230ºC (400-450ºF)

Ingredients	Metric	Imperial
Eggs	4	4
Freshly ground pepper	to season	to season
Anchovy fillets	4	4
Mozzarella cheese	60 g	2 oz
Anchovy paste	¼ teaspoon	¼ teaspoon
Melted butter	1 tablespoon	1 tablespoon

Grease 4 ramekin dishes and break an egg into each. Grind pepper over each egg and place anchovy fillets on top. Thinly slice cheese and place a slice on each egg. Blend anchovy paste with butter, stirring well to mix, then sprinkle over cheese. Bake in a hot oven for 8-10 minutes, or until eggs are just set and cheese has melted.

Note: Anchovy paste from France and Italy, is manufactured in tubes and is available from delicatessens. Mashed canned anchovies can be used in place of paste. If a milder anchovy taste is preferred, anchovies can be washed and dried to remove excess salt.

OMELETTE

Frittata
Serves: 4

Ingredients	Metric	Imperial
Eggs	6	6
Salt and pepper	to season	to season
Olive oil	2 tablespoons	2 tablespoons

Beat eggs until just mixed and season with salt and pepper. Heat 1 tablespoon oil in a heavy frying pan, pour in eggs and cook over a low heat until underside is set and golden brown. Hold a plate over top of pan and turn omelette on to it. Heat remaining oil in pan, then slide omelette back into pan to cook and brown the other side. Slip on to a plate and serve flat.

Variations: Omelettes are often flavoured with a few spoonsful of chopped ham, cooked prawns, baby clams, diced cheese (packaged cream cheese makes a delicious creamy omelette) or chopped fresh herbs. Add the flavourings to beaten eggs and proceed as above.

OMELETTE WITH BREAD CUBES

Serves: 2-3

Ingredients	Metric	Imperial
Bread	2 slices	2 slices
Mozzarella cheese	125 g	4 oz
Eggs	4	4
Salt and pepper	to season	to season
Butter	30 g	1 oz

Cut bread into cubes and finely dice cheese. Beat eggs until just mixed, season with salt and pepper and stir in diced cheese.

Heat butter in a frying pan and fry bread cubes, turning frequently, until golden brown on all sides. Pour in egg mixture and cook over a low heat until underside of omelette is set and golden, then place plate on top of pan and turn omelette on to it. Slide omelette back into pan and cook until underside is golden. Serve flat, cut in wedges.

FRIED EGGS WITH CHEESE

Uova al Tegame al Formaggio
Serves: 4

Ingredients	Metric	Imperial
Butter	30 g	1 oz
Ham	4 slices	4 slices
Bel paese or mozzarella cheese	125 g	4 oz
Eggs	8	8

It is preferable to use 4 individual, shallow fireproof dishes and serve straight from stove to table, but a frying pan can be used.

Melt butter in the dishes, and when hot put in ham and top with slices of cheese. Break 2 eggs into each dish. Cover with lids or aluminium foil and cook very gently until eggs are set. A high heat will cause ham and cheese to burn.

Note: Ham can be omitted if wished.

Variations: Ham and cheese may be cut into julienne (matchstick size) strips and sprinkled on top of eggs in dishes.

VEGETABLES

VEGETABLES

In Italy, vegetables appear on the table at every meal. Even at breakfast, sliced tomatoes with herbs and oil sprinkled over, are eaten with bread for the first meal of the day in southern Italy.

They are rarely served as an accompaniment to meat and poultry — the exception being a grill or roast, when one or two potatoes and a green salad may be served.

Italians enjoy vegetables raw as salads with a little vinaigrette dressing. They are partial also to cooked vegetables which are allowed to cool, then dressed with a squeeze of lemon juice, salt and a grind of black pepper. Many vegetables are fried, others are blended together with cheese or fresh tomato sauce. Some are filled with seasonings and baked. A great many vegetables are treated as a separate dish, usually as a first course.

Fennel or finnochio, globe artichokes, eggplant, slender young green zucchini, red and green capsicums, with their brilliant colours and plump shapes, all dominate market stalls and green-grocer displays all over the world. They stand with their so Italian names as evidence that Italy is indeed the land of vegetables.

EGGPLANT PARMIGIANA

Serves: 4
Cooking time: 15 minutes
Oven temperature: 200-230°C (400-450°F)

Ingredients	Metric	Imperial
Eggplant	1 large	1 large
Olive oil	250 ml	1 cup
Tomato Sauce (see page 49)	315 ml	1¼ cups
Grated parmesan cheese	3 tablespoons	3 tablespoons
Mozarella cheese, thinly sliced	250 g	8 oz

Peel eggplant and cut in thin slices. Fry in oil until brown and drain on kitchen paper. Place a layer of fried eggplant in an ovenproof casserole, cover with Tomato Sauce, sprinkle with parmesan cheese and cover with a layer of mozarella cheese. Repeat layers until all the ingredients are used, ending with a layer of mozarella. Bake in a hot oven for 15 minutes. Serve hot.

POTATOES PARMIGIANA

Serves: 4
Cooking time: approximately 20 minutes
Oven temperature: 200-230°C (400-450°F)

Ingredients	Metric	Imperial
Potatoes	4 medium sized	4 medium sized
Butter	30 g	1 oz
Strong stock	1 tablespoon	1 tablespoon
Pepper	¼ teaspoon	¼ teaspoon
Extra butter, melted	2 tablespoons	2 tablespoons
Grated parmesan cheese	3 tablespoons	3 tablespoons

Peel and finely dice potatoes. Cook in butter until tender, about 7 minutes. Add stock. Turn into a greased baking dish, sprinkle with salt, pepper, melted butter and cheese. Bake in a hot oven for 10 minutes.

BROCCOLI ROMAN STYLE

Serves: 4

Ingredients	Metric	Imperial
Broccoli	1 small bunch	1 small bunch
Olive oil	60 ml	¼ cup
Garlic, sliced	2 cloves	2 cloves
Salt	½ teaspoon	½ teaspoon
Pepper	½ teaspoon	½ teaspoon
Dry red wine	375 ml	1½ cups

Cut off tough outer leaves from broccoli, trim stems, then cut into small flowerets. Wash well and drain. Place olive oil and garlic in a large frying pan and brown garlic. Add broccoli, salt and pepper and cook 5 minutes. Add wine, cover pan and cook over a very low heat for 20 minutes, or until broccoli is tender, stirring gently to prevent breaking flowerets.

BRAISED FENNEL

Serves: 4

Ingredients	Metric	Imperial
Fennel	3 small bulbs	3 small bulbs
Olive oil	60 ml	¼ cup
Garlic, sliced	1 clove	1 clove
Chopped basil	½ teaspoon	½ teaspoon
Chopped mint leaves	¼ teaspoon	¼ teaspoon
Salt	½ teaspoon	½ teaspoon
Pepper	½ teaspoon	½ teaspoon

Cut tops off fennel almost level with bulb. Wash well and slice, not too finely. Place in a saucepan with oil, garlic, basil, mint, salt and pepper. Cover pan and cook over a low heat for 1 hour, stirring occasionally.

PEPERONATA CONTADINA

Serves: 6-8

Ingredients	Metric	Imperial
Eggplant	2	2
Coarse salt	2 teaspoons	2 teaspoons
Olive oil	125 ml	½ cup
Onions	2 large	2 large
Green capsicum	1	1
Red capsicum	1	1
Tomatoes	3 large	3 large
Zucchini	4 small	4 small
Plain flour	for coating	for coating
Salt and pepper	to taste	to taste

Slice eggplant 5 mm (¼-inch) thick. Place on a large plate, sprinkle with coarse salt and cover with a heavy plate. Leave 30 minutes to extract all the bitterness and excess water. Rinse eggplant under cold water, drain and spread slices on kitchen paper to dry.

Heat 3 tablespoons olive oil in a large pan, add sliced onions and capsicums which have been seeded and cut in thin strips, cook slowly until soft.

Meanwhile, cut tomatoes in wedges and zucchini in diagonal slices. Toss slices of eggplant in flour and coat well. Heat remaining oil in a pan and briskly sauté eggplant in oil, turning, until browned and crisp. Drain on paper towels. Fry 3-4 slices at a time.

Add eggplant, tomato and zucchini to softened onion and capsicum. Season to taste with salt and pepper. Cover pan and cook slowly for 1 hour or more, stirring occasionally.

Serve hot as a vegetable accompaniment or as part of an antipasto tray. May also be served cold. Excellent with grilled and roasted meats.

ARTICHOKES (see page 67)

Variations: Peperonata with Eggs: Place a generous layer of peperonata in an ovenproof dish and make a series of hollows in the surface with a spoon. Carefully slip a raw egg into each depression and sprinkle 2 tablespoons chopped black olives over. Bake in a moderate oven 170-190°C (350-375°F) for 30-35 minutes. Serve hot or cold as an antipasto or as a light luncheon dish.

Peperonato with Pasta: Spread a layer of cooked macaroni in a baking dish and cover with peperonata. Moisten with a little Béchamel Sauce (see page 47) which has been flavoured with a little grated parmesan or mozzarella cheese. Repeat layers until dish is full, heat in a moderate oven 170-190°C (350-375°F) for 30 minutes. Serve immediately.

STUFFED TOMATOES

Pomodori Ripieni
Serves: 6
Cooking time: 20 minutes
Oven temperature: 190-200°C (375-400°F)

Ingredients	Metric	Imperial
Tomatoes	6 medium sized	6 medium sized
Tuna in oil	1 x 205 g can	1 x 6½ oz can
Bread	3 slices	3 slices
Anchovy fillets, chopped	6	6
Garlic, crushed	1 clove	1 clove
Dried basil	½ teaspoon	½ teaspoon
Fine dry breadcrumbs	2 tablespoons	2 tablespoons
Grated parmesan cheese	1½ tablespoons	1½ tablespoons
Melted butter	3 tablespoons	3 tablespoons

Remove and discard tops of tomatoes. Scoop out pulp, push through a coarse sieve and mix thoroughly with tuna, coarsely crumbled bread (crusts removed), anchovy fillets, garlic and basil. Divide filling between tomatoes. Sprinkle top of tomatoes with breadcrumbs, cheese and melted butter mixed together.

Arrange stuffed tomatoes in an oiled baking dish and bake in a moderately hot oven for about 20 minutes, or until they are heated through and topping is brown.

PEAS WITH PROSCIUTTO ROMAN STYLE

Serves: 4

Ingredients	Metric	Imperial
Butter	60 g	2 oz
Onion, sliced	1 small	1 small
Shelled fresh or frozen peas	500 ml	2 cups
Salt	¾ teaspoon	¾ teaspoon
Pepper	½ teaspoon	½ teaspoon
Stock or water	2 tablespoons	2 tablespoons
Prosciutto or ham, shredded	6 slices	6 slices
Sugar	¼ teaspoon	¼ teaspoon

Melt butter in a saucepan and cook sliced onion until brown. Add peas, salt, pepper and stock and cook briskly for 10 minutes, stirring frequently. Add shredded prosciutto, lower heat and cook until peas are tender, about 10 minutes, depending on peas. Add sugar and a little more stock if required, and serve.

MUSHROOMS

Funghi

Mushrooms of all shapes and flavours are featured in meals throughout Italy. Both field and cultivated mushrooms respond to this simple treatment, and are especially good with the addition of oregano, that most Italian of herbs.

Serves: 4

Ingredients	Metric	Imperial
Mushrooms	1 kg	2 lb
Olive oil	250 ml	1 cup
Garlic	2 cloves	2 cloves
Dried oregano	good pinch	good pinch
Salt	to taste	to taste

Wipe mushrooms with a clean damp cloth. Remove stalks and slice caps. Heat oil in a frying pan and add 1 whole clove and 1 crushed clove garlic. Lower heat. Sprinkle mushrooms with oregano and seaon to taste with salt. Continue cooking over a low heat until mushrooms are tender, approximately 10 minutes.

Serve as a first course with crusty bread or serve as a vegetable with roast chicken or a grill.

ARTICHOKES

Carciofi
Serves: 4

Ingredients	Metric	Imperial
Globe artichokes	4 medium sized	4 medium sized
Olive oil	2 tablespoons	2 tablespoons
Dry white wine	125 ml	½ cup
Garlic, finely chopped	2 cloves	2 cloves
Onion, finely chopped	1 small	1 small
Finely chopped parsley	1 tablespoon	1 tablespoon
Dried savory	pinch	pinch
Salt and freshly ground	to taste	to taste
pepper	to taste	to taste
Vinaigrette Dressing (see page 11)		

Remove tough outer leaves of artichokes and trim tops off inner leaves. Trim base and stem of each artichoke with a sharp knife. Combine oil, wine, garlic, onion, parsley, savory, salt and freshly ground pepper to taste and put into a saucepan with artichokes. Cover pan tightly and simmer slowly for 45 minutes, adding a little more oil and wine if necessary. Artichokes are cooked when a leaf pulls out easily. Turn upside down to drain. Serve cold with Vinaigrette Dressing. Pull off a leaf at a time and eat the tender base of each leaf. Remove hairy choke with a spoon and eat artichoke heart.

STUFFED ZUCCHINI

Serves: 4
Cooking time: 35 minutes
Oven temperature: 170-190°C (350-375°F)

Ingredients	Metric	Imperial
Zucchini	8 small	8 small
Minced steak	250 g	8 oz
Egg	1	1
Grated parmesan cheese	2 tablespoons	2 tablespoons
Bread, soaked in water and squeezed dry	1 slice	1 slice
Bacon rasher, shredded	1	1
Salt	½ teaspoon	½ teaspoon
Pepper	½ teaspoon	½ teaspoon
Oil	2 teaspoons	2 teaspoons
Butter	15 g	½ oz
Onion, chopped	1 very small	1 very small
Chopped parsley	2 teaspoons	2 teaspoons
Tomato paste	2 tablespoons	2 tablespoons
Water	250 ml	1 cup

With an apple corer, remove inside flesh of zucchini, taking care not to break the skins. Mix minced steak, egg, parmesan cheese, bread, bacon, salt and pepper together thoroughly. Stuff zucchini with mixture.

Heat oil and butter in a large flameproof casserole and add onion and parsley. Brown well. Add tomato paste and water and cook for 5 minutes. Place zucchini in sauce. If sauce is not enough to cover zucchini, add water. Bake in a moderate oven for 30 minutes.

RICE, BEANS AND OTHER SPECIALITIES

RICE, BEANS AND OTHER SPECIALITIES

Rice cooked the Italian way is utterly delicious — no wonder it is served as a separate dish, it would be a shame to spoil it by sharing it with other foods.

Other specialities like gnocchi and beans, and pizza — that most Italian of all foods, are popular all over the world and have done much to build up our picture of what constitutes Italian food.

Italians take great care with everything they cook, the best and freshest ingredients are used. Although they can, like good French cooks, be frugal, the dish is never spoiled for the want of the right ingredient.

Risotto is best made with Italian short grain rice which is available in many Italian delicatessen shops. When making it, it is important not to skimp on such things as saffron. Also don't be dismayed at the ingredients for canneloni — this version takes time but is well worth it even if you only make it once a year.

Home-made pizza is really quite simple to make, and is a vast improvement on the bought variety.

Try too the light little morsels of poached potato gnocchi — or the golden semolina gnocchi — a speciality from the north. Just serve them with a light green salad, for a perfect simple luncheon.

SEMOLINA CAKES WITH BUTTER AND CHEESE

Gnocchi alla Romana
Serves: 4
Cooking time: 15 minutes
Oven temperature: 170-190°C (350-375°F)

Ingredients	Metric	Imperial
Onion	1	1
Bay leaf	1	1
Milk	935 ml	3¾ cups
Semolina or cornmeal	185 ml	¾ cup
Salt	1½ teaspoons	1½ teaspoons
Pepper	to taste	to taste
Grated parmesan cheese	90 g	3 oz
Butter	60 g	2 oz
Dry mustard	½ teaspoon	½ teaspoon

Peel onion, cut in half and put in a saucepan with bay leaf and milk. Bring slowly to the boil, remove onion and bay leaf, add semolina, salt and pepper. Cook, stirring over a low heat for 15-20 minutes or until very thick. Remove from heat, stir in half the grated cheese, 15 g (½ oz) butter and the mustard. Spread out on an oiled baking tray to an oblong slightly less than 10 mm (½-inch) thick. Cool. When cold, cut into circles with a 5 cm (2-inch) cutter or in squares with a knife.

Arrange circles of gnocchi, slightly overlapping, in a well-oiled shallow ovenproof dish. Sprinkle with remaining cheese. Melt remaining butter and sprinkle over top. Bake in a moderate oven for 15 minutes, then place under a hot grill until top is brown and crisp. Serve immediately, while still bubbling.

Serve as a luncheon dish with salad or as an accompaniment to a grill or roast chicken.

RICE WITH SAFFRON

Risotto alla Milanese

Risotto in Italy is served before the main course with one exception — it often accompanies osso buco. It is also delicious served with mushrooms or chicken livers. The distinctive difference Risotto alla Milanese has is the addition of saffron. When making risotto, the liquid is added slowly and it must be absorbed after each addition. This method of cooking rice results in a creamy rice with each grain still separate. Look for the short fat Italian rice sold in many Italian delicatessens.

Serves: 4

Ingredients	Metric	Imperial
Chicken stock	1.5 litre	6 cups
Saffron	good pinch	good pinch
Onion	1 small	1 small
Butter	125 g	4 oz
Short grain rice	500 g	1 lb
Marsala	125 ml	½ cup
Grated parmesan cheese	250 ml	1 cup

Bring chicken stock (or water and stock cubes) to the boil and keep hot. Take out 250 ml (1 cup) and steep the saffron. Chop onion finely.

In a heavy saucepan, melt 90 g (3 oz) butter, add onion and cook gently, stirring, until beginning to colour. Do not brown. Add unwashed rice and stir for 3-4 minutes. Stir in marsala and when evaporated, add 125 ml (½ cup) of the boiling stock. Cook over a medium heat, uncovered, until stock is absorbed. Add remaining stock gradually, stirring constantly, and lastly add saffron steeped stock. When rice is tender, add remaining butter and the cheese. Stir lightly. Serve immediately while rice is creamy and hot with extra grated parmesan cheese if liked.

Note: For a very rich flavour, butter can be reduced to 60 g (2 oz) and 60 g (2 oz) beef marrow can be added with the onion.

Ask your butcher to split the marrow bones lengthways to make it easier to remove the marrow. Marsala can be replaced by white wine.

The amount of chicken stock required may vary, according to the type of rice used, but the result should be creamy, not sloppy.

BEANS

Fagioli
Serves: 4-6

Ingredients	Metric	Imperial
Cannelini beans	500 g	1 lb
Carrot	1 small	1 small
Celery	2 stalks	2 stalks
Fat bacon	90 g	3 oz
Salt	to season	to season
Olive oil	2 tablespoons	2 tablespoons

Soak beans in cold water to cover overnight. Drain beans and put into a heavy saucepan with carrot, cut lengthways in 4; celery, cut in short strips; and diced bacon. Season with salt. Add enough cold water to cover the ingredients. Bring to the boil and simmer for 1 hour, or until beans are tender. Drain water off and sprinkle beans with olive oil before serving.

BASIC PIZZA

Makes: 2 large pizzas, cut each into 8 wedges
Cooking time: 20 minutes
Oven temperature: 200-230°C (400-450°F)

Ingredients	Metric	Imperial
Luke-warm water	250 ml	1 cup
Compressed yeast	30 g	1 oz
Olive oil	3 tablespoons	3 tablespoons
Plain flour	750 ml	3 cups
Salt	1½ teaspoons	1½ teaspoons
White pepper	to taste	to taste
Tomato Sauce (see page 49)	500 ml	2 cups
Grated mozzarella cheese	250 ml	1 cup
Grated parmesan cheese	4 tablespoons	4 tablespoons
Extra olive oil	2 tablespoons	2 tablespoons

Pour water into a large warm bowl. Crumble yeast into water and stir until smooth. Stir in olive oil. Sift flour, salt and pepper over yeast mixture. Blend thoroughly with a spoon. Turn on to a lightly floured surface and knead gently until dough is smooth and elastic.

Place in a large greased bowl, turn dough to grease surface all over and cover with a tea towel. Leave in a warm place until double in bulk, about 2 hours.

Knead dough on a lightly floured board 4-5 times. Divide in half. Roll out each portion to a circle, 30 cm (12-inches) in diameter and 5 mm (¼-inch) thick. Press out to edge of greased pizza pans (do not cut).

Spoon 250 ml (1 cup) Tomato Sauce over each pizza and spread over surface with the back of a spoon. Sprinkle sauce with grated mozzarella and parmesan cheese, and finally with oil. Bake in a hot oven for 20 minutes or until crust is lightly browned and cheese bubbling.

Alternative Garnishes: Always start by spreading Tomato Sauce over pizza and then top with any kind of seafood, meat or vegetable with cheese (optional) then finish off with a light sprinkling of olive oil.

Select from these garnishes:
- Prawns, black olives and capers.
- Anchovy fillets, black olives and mozzarella cheese.
- Black and green olives with peperoni (preserved capsicums), prawns, mushrooms and prosciutto.
- Salami strips or slices with olives, anchovy fillets and green or red capsicum.
- Prosciutto slices with olives and mushrooms.
- Green and red capsicum with anchovy fillets, olives, prawns or salami.
- Capers with anchovy fillets, black olives and prawns.
- Whole or sliced mushrooms with prosciutto, olives, green or red capsicum or capers.

The ingredients for pizza toppings may be varied to suit yourself. They may be lavish or simple, and may or may not be sprinkled with cheese. Choose the particular combination which suits the occasion.

HARICOT BEANS WITH SAGE

Fagioli all'uccelletto
Serves: 6

Ingredients	Metric	Imperial
Dried haricot beans	500 g	1 lb
Olive oil	185 ml	¾ cup
Garlic, bruised	2 cloves	2 cloves
Sage	1 sprig	1 sprig
Whole tomatoes	1 x 500 g can	1 x 16 oz can
Salt and pepper	to taste	to taste

Soak beans in cold water overnight, then cook in lightly salted water for about 2 hours, or until tender. Drain. Heat oil in a large saucepan. Fry garlic until brown, then discard. Add beans, sage and drained and chopped tomatoes. Season with salt and freshly ground pepper and cook for 20 minutes or until sauce is thick. Remove sage.

CANNELONI

Canneloni in Italian means 'big pipes'. The noodles are shaped like big tubes or flat sheets which are rolled up, and are available from many shops. But many favour a fine pancake which is filled, rolled up and coated with a sauce before baking. There are many fillings for Canneloni, the following being one of my favourites.

Serves: 8
Cooking time: 30 minutes
Oven temperature: 170-190°C (350-375°F)

Ingredients	Metric	Imperial
Pancakes:		
Plain flour	250 ml	1 cup
Grated nutmeg	pinch	pinch
Salt	½ teaspoon	½ teaspoon
Pepper	pinch	pinch
Eggs	3	3
Milk	375 ml	1½ cups
Melted butter	2 teaspoons	2 teaspoons
Brandy	2 teaspoons	2 teaspoons
Extra butter for cooking		
Filling:		
Chicken breasts	750 g	1½ lb
Chicken livers	250 g	8 oz
Butter	125 g	4 oz
Prosciutto or ham	125 g	4 oz
Mozzarella cheese, grated	125 g	4 oz
Grated parmesan cheese	6 tablespoons	6 tablespoons
Plain flour	4 tablespoons	4 tablespoons
Milk	1 litre	4 cups
Cream	125 ml	½ cup
Salt and pepper	to taste	to taste
Grated nutmeg	good pinch	good pinch

Pancakes: Sift flour, nutmeg, salt and pepper into a mixing bowl. Make a well in the centre. Combine lightly beaten eggs and milk and pour into well. Stir gradually, incorporating flour until batter is smooth. Add butter and brandy. Cover and allow to stand for 1 hour.

Grease a shallow frying pan with a little butter and, when sizzling, pour in sufficient batter to cover base of pan with a thin layer. Rotate pan quickly to spread batter as thinly and evenly as possible. When golden, turn over and cook other side. Stack pancakes flat between squares of greaseproof paper. You will need 16 pancakes, each about 18 cm (7-inches) in diameter. Wrap any extra pancakes in aluminium foil and freeze.

Filling: Remove bones and skin from chicken breasts. Halve chicken livers. Melt 60 g (2 oz) butter in a pan and sauté chicken breasts over a moderate heat until golden and cooked through, about 10 minutes. Push to one side of pan, add chicken livers and cook for 4 minutes, turning them. Mince chicken meat and livers with prosciutto, or chop finely. Mix together with mozzarella cheese and 2 tablespoons of the parmesan cheese.

Melt remaining butter in a large saucepan, add flour and stir for 2 minutes. Add milk and stir until sauce boils and thickens. Lower heat and cook 5 minutes, stirring. Add cream, salt, pepper and freshly grated nutmeg. Blend 250 ml (1 cup) of sauce with minced chicken mixture.

Spoon about 2 tablespoons filling on each pancake and roll up tightly. Spoon a little of the reserved sauce into a large shallow ovenproof dish and place Canneloni on top in one layer. Coat with remaining sauce and sprinkle with remaining parmesan cheese. Bake in a moderate oven for about 30 minutes, or until golden.

Note: If using packaged canneloni tubes, cook them in a large saucepan of boiling salted water for about 12 minutes, or until tender. Drain thoroughly and dry on a clean cloth. Spoon or pipe filling into tubes. Quantity of filling is enough for 16 tubes.

POTATO GNOCCHI ROMAN STYLE

Gnocchi di Patate
Serves: 6

Ingredients	Metric	Imperial
Old potatoes	2 kg	4 lb
Salt	2 teaspoons	2 teaspoons
Eggs	2	2
Plain flour	about 750 ml	about 3 cups
Bolognese Sauce (see page 48)	1 quantity	1 quantity
Grated parmesan cheese for serving		

Dough for potato gnocchi is best prepared just before cooking as it becomes damp if allowed to stand.

Peel potatoes, cut into even sized pieces and put into a large saucepan with water to cover. Add salt, bring to the boil and cook for 20 minutes or until tender. Drain well and mash potatoes until smooth, or push through a coarse sieve. Taste and add more salt if necessary. While still warm, add slightly beaten eggs. Work in enough sifted flour to make a firm but soft dough. It may be necessary to add more flour, depending on moisteness of potato.

Divide dough into pieces and roll in well-floured hands to thick pencil shapes about 10 mm (½-inch) in diameter. Cut into 2.5 cm (1-inch) lengths and pinch the centre of each one lightly between finger and thumb. Place them on a lightly floured tea towel. Make sure they do not touch each other and stick together.

Bring a large saucepan of salted water to a rapid boil and drop in gnocchi a few at a time. Do not crowd the pan. As soon as gnocchi float to the surface, remove with a slotted spoon. When all are cooked and drained, stir into sauce and serve topped with grated parmesan cheese.

Note: Potato gnocchi can be served simply tossed with melted butter and grated parmesan cheese, or with Tomato Sauce (see page 49) instead of Bolognese Sauce.

RICE WITH PEAS

Risi e Bisi

Although considered a soup by Italians, this dish is so thick it is eaten with a fork.

Serves: 4-6

Ingredients	Metric	Imperial
Butter	60 g	2 oz
Olive oil	2 tablespoons	2 tablespoons
Lean bacon rashers	2	2
Shallots	3	3
Shelled peas	750 ml	3 cups
Chicken stock	2.5 litres	4 pints
Rice	440 ml	1¾ cups
Salt	to taste	to taste
Finely chopped parsley	2 tablespoons	2 tablespoons
Grated parmesan cheese for serving		

Heat butter and oil in a large saucepan, gently sauté diced bacon and finely sliced shallots until bacon browns. Add peas and 3 tablespoons stock and cook gently for about 15 minutes. Add remaining stock and rice, bring to the boil, stir well. Lower heat and cook gently until rice is tender and fairly moist, 20-25 minutes. Add salt to taste. Serve at once while the rice is creamy and hot, sprinkled with parsley. Serve grated parmesan cheese separately.

RISOTTO WITH MUSHROOMS

Rissoto con Funghi
Serves: 6

Ingredients	Metric	Imperial
Mushrooms	250 g	8 oz
Bacon rashers	2	2
Onion	1 small	1 small
Butter	60 g	2 oz
Garlic	1 clove	1 clove
Finely chopped parsley	2 tablespoons	2 tablespoons
Rice	750 ml	3 cups
Chicken stock	about 2 litres	about 8 cups
Salt and pepper	to taste	to taste
Grated parmesan cheese	6 tablespoons	6 tablespoons

Slice mushrooms, finely chop bacon and onion. Melt butter in large saucepan and sauté bacon and onion with garlic. When onion is golden, add mushrooms and parsley. Cook over a low heat for a few minutes, then discard garlic and add rice. Fry for 5 minutes, stirring constantly, then add 250 ml (1 cup) boiling stock and cook until it is absorbed. Continue cooking and adding stock a cupful at a time, until rice is tender and all liquid is absorbed. Add salt and pepper to taste, stir in cheese and leave risotto over a low heat for a few minutes before serving.

Note: Risotto may be prepared in this way using other vegetables. Shelled prawns, mussels or slivers of chicken meat may also be added with the mushrooms.

CHICKEN WITH CAPSICUMS (see page 87)

PAN FRIED SQUID (see page 91)

CHICKEN AND FISH

CHICKEN AND FISH

Chicken cacciatora is one of the best known and loved chicken dishes and appears in homes and restaurants throughout the world. Literally it means 'hunter style', an indication that the bird is cooked in the simple ingredients to be found in the fields.

Another favourite is grilled chicken which is split in two and simply seared over a charcoal fire. The bird must be young and very plump. It is often finished off with just a hint of lemon juice, salt and freshly ground pepper.

With today's mass production of poultry we are often left with an inexpensive but rather tasteless bird. Chicken cooked the Italian way with flavoursome vegetables, herbs and spices, is delicious and rich. Serve plenty of crusty Italian bread to mop up the juices.

The abundance and variety of Mediterranean seafoods encourages fish eating habits.

Often the best dishes are the simplest ones. Sea-fresh fish grilled or fried needs no complicated sauces, for the Italians are content with their skill in the art of grilling or frying. They have also developed other skills and seem to have the knack of obtaining added flavour from basic foods without overshadowing the natural flavour. This is nowhere more apparent than in their fish cookery.

Interesting fish stews and soups, roast fish, baked fish and fish fries (fritto misto di pesce) abound throughout Italy.

CHICKEN CACCIATORA

Pollo alla Cacciatora — 'Hunter Style'
Serves: 6

Ingredients	Metric	Imperial
Chickens	2 x 1.25 kg	2 x 2½ lb
Plain flour	8 tablespoons	8 tablespoons
Salt and pepper	to season	to season
Green capsicum	1	1
Onion	1	1
Garlic	2 cloves	2 cloves
Olive oil	3 tablespoons	3 tablespoons
Tomatoes	4-6	4-6
Bay leaf	1	1
Dry white wine	125 ml	½ cup
Chopped parsley	1 tablespoon	1 tablespoon
Black olives	6	6
Green olives	6	6

Cut chickens into serving pieces and coat with flour seasoned with salt and freshly ground pepper. Remove seeds and membrane from capsicum and cut into dice, chop onion and crush garlic. Heat oil in a heavy pan and fry chicken gently until golden on all sides, placing chicken in pan one layer at a time. Remove chicken. If necessary, add a little more oil to pan and fry capsicum, onion and garlic until onion is golden. Add peeled tomatoes, bay leaf, 1 teaspoon salt and a good grinding of pepper. Bring to the boil, simmer for a few minutes, then return chicken to pan. Add wine, cover and simmer gently for about 30 minutes, or until chicken is tender. Garnish with parsley and stoned olives.

Note: Drained canned tomatoes may replace fresh.

BREAST OF CHICKEN EN PAPILLOTE

Filetti di Pollo al Cartoccio
Serves: 4
Cooking time: 5 minutes
Oven temperature: 200-230ºC (400-450ºF)

Ingredients	Metric	Imperial
Bolognese Sauce (see page 48)	185 ml	¾ cup
Greaseproof paper	4 sheets	4 sheets
Olive oil	for greasing	for greasing
Chicken breasts	4	4
Salt and pepper	to season	to season
Plain flour	2 tablespoons	2 tablespoons
Butter	60 g	2 oz
Prosciutto or ham	8 thin slices	8 thin slices

Prepare Bolognese Sauce. Cut greaseproof paper into heart shaped pieces large enough to encase chicken breasts when paper is folded in half. Brush both sides of paper with a little oil. Bone chicken breasts, then season with salt and pepper and sprinkle lightly with flour. Heat butter in a frying pan and quickly sauté chicken one layer at a time, over a high heat, allowing 3 minutes on each side. Butter should be hot enough to brown chicken in this time.

Place a slice of prosciutto on one half of each paper heart, top with chicken breast and spoon Bolognese Sauce over. Top with remaining slice of prosciutto. Fold other half of the paper heart over chicken and seal edges by crimping. Place on a baking tray and put into a hot oven for about 5 minutes or until paper is puffed and browned. Serve immediately.

FRIED CHICKEN FLORENTINE

Pollo Fritto Fiorentina

The best chickens in Italy come from Tuscany. The young,
plump tender birds are marinated and cooked in the simplest
of ways, over a charcoal grill or fried, as in this recipe.

Serves: 4

Ingredients	Metric	Imperial
Chicken	1 x 1.75 kg	1 x 3½ lb
Olive oil	3 tablespoons	3 tablespoons
Lemon juice	2 tablespoons	2 tablespoons
Salt	½ teaspoon	½ teaspoon
Pepper	to taste	to taste
Chopped parsley	1 tablespoon	1 tablespoon
Plain flour	for coating	for coating
Egg	1	1
Extra oil	for frying	for frying

Cut chicken into serving pieces. Combine oil, lemon juice,
salt, pepper and parsley and marinate chicken in mixture for
2 hours, turning pieces occasionally.

Dry chicken thoroughly, coat well with flour, then dip into
slightly beaten egg and fry in deep hot oil for about 15
minutes, or until chicken is tender and cooked through.
Drain on paper towels and serve hot.

CHICKEN MACERATA STYLE

Pollo alla Maceratese
Serves: 4

Ingredients	Metric	Imperial
Chicken	1 x 1.25 kg	1 x 2½ lb
Salt	to season	to season
Olive oil	6 tablespoons	6 tablespoons
Butter	60 g	2 oz
Chicken stock	500 ml	2 cups
Egg yolks	2	2
Lemon juice	2 tablespoons	2 tablespoons

Remove neck and giblets, if any, from chicken and season cavity with salt. Heat oil and butter in a heavy flameproof casserole (preferably oval) large enough to fit chicken snugly. Add giblets and neck and sauté for 2 minutes. Add chicken and cook, turning occasionally with two large spoons, until golden on all sides. Add stock (there should be enough to almost cover chicken). Cook covered, over a very low heat for about 1 hour or until chicken is tender. Remove lid and cook over a high heat to reduce sauce.

Lift chicken from casserole and cut into serving pieces. Arrange on a serving platter and keep warm. Beat egg yolks until thoroughly combines, but not frothy, add lemon juice and then stir into sauce in casserole. Continue stirring over a low heat for 1 minute or just until sauce thickens. Remove from heat and add more salt if necessary to taste. Pour over chicken and serve immediately.

CHICKEN WITH CAPSICUMS

Spezzantini di Pollo con Peperoni

Chickens get special treatment in Italy. Tomatoes and strips of green capsicum, wine and olive oil, bring a new dimension to fried chicken.

Serves: 6

Ingredients	Metric	Imperial
Chickens	2 x 1.25 kg	2 x 2½ lb
Olive oil	4-5 tablespoons	4-5 tablespoons
Salt and pepper	to season	to season
Onion	1 small	1 small
Dry white wine	185 ml	¾ cup
Ripe tomatoes	500 g	1 lb
Green capsicums	4	4
Garlic	1 clove	1 clove

Cut chickens into serving pieces. In a large frying pan heat 2 tablespoons oil and sauté chicken, skin side down first, until golden on both sides, adding a little more oil to pan if needed. Cook chicken one layer at a time. Season with salt and pepper to taste. Add finely chopped onion and wine, and cook until wine is reduced by half. Add tomatoes which have been peeled, seeded and chopped. Cover pan with lid or transfer contents to a heavy flameproof casserole with a lid, and cook gently for 20 minutes.

Discard seeds and membrane from capsicums and cut into strips. Heat remaining oil in a saucepan and stir in crushed garlic and capsicum strips. Sauté for a few minutes, then add to chicken. Cover and cook gently for a further 10 minutes or until chicken is tender. Serve with thick slices of crusty bread and a tossed salad.

CHICKEN WITH EGGPLANT

Pollo Spezzato e Melanzane
Serves: 4

Ingredients	Metric	Imperial
Chicken	1 x 1.5 kg	1 x 3 lb
Small eggplants	4	4
Salt and pepper	to season	to season
Olive oil	250 ml	1 cup
Garlic	1 clove	1 clove
Dry white wine	250 ml	1 cup
Ripe tomatoes	500 g	1 lb
Ham fat or streaky bacon	125 g	4 oz
Chicken stock or water	to moisten	to moisten
Finely chopped parsley	1 tablespoon	1 tablespoon

Cut chicken into 4 even sized pieces. Wash eggplants, but do not peel. Cut into small pieces, place in a colander sprinkling each layer with salt. Put a plate on top and leave for 1 hour, then drain off juice, wash eggplant and wipe dry.

Heat 85 ml (1/3 cup) oil in a heavy flameproof casserole or saucepan and sauté bruised garlic until brown, then discard. Add chicken to pan (in 2 lots if necessary) and fry until evenly golden all over. Sprinkle with salt and pepper, then add wine and cook over a moderate heat, uncovered, until wine evaporates.

Peel and chop tomatoes, discarding seeds. Add tomato to chicken with finely chopped ham fat. Cover and cook gently for 30 minutes. If sauce in pan is dry, add a little stock to moisten.

Heat remaining oil in a separate pan, add well drained eggplant. Sprinkle generously with freshly ground pepper and fry 15 minutes, adding parsley for last 5 minutes of cooking time.

Add to chicken in casserole, taste and season with salt and pepper if necessary. Stir gently to mix and allow to heat through. Serve very hot.

FRESH TUNA WITH PEAS

Tonno Fresco con Piselli
Serves: 4

Ingredients	Metric	Imperial
Fresh peas in pod	1 kg	2 lb
or frozen peas	375 g	12 oz
Fresh tuna or any firm flesh fish	1 kg	2 lb
Garlic	2 cloves	2 cloves
Olive oil	125 ml	½ cup
Salt	1 teaspoon	1 teaspoon
Ground pepper	½ teaspoon	½ teaspoon
Tomato paste	2 tablespoons	2 tablespoons
Water	250 ml	1 cup
Chopped parsley	2 tablespoons	2 tablespoons

Shell fresh peas. Cut tuna into 2.5 cm (1-inch) thick slices and dry on paper towels. Hit garlic with blade of a heavy knife and discard skin. Heat garlic with oil in a frying pan and when garlic turns golden, remove and discard. Add tuna to oil, sprinkle with salt and pepper, and when golden turn and brown other side.

Blend tomato paste with water and add to pan. Simmer until tuna is cooked, then lift tuna slices out of pan and keep warm. Add peas to sauce in pan and cook over a low heat until tender. Young fresh peas will take about 10 minutes, frozen about 4 minutes. If sauce becomes dry, add a little more water. Return tuna to pan, sprinkle with parsley and season with more salt and pepper if necessary. When heated through, serve.

FRIED MIXED FISH

Fritto Misto di Pesce

Small seafood fries vary from region to region but always the batter is crisp and light, and if you detect a distinctive flavour, it may be the unusual use of herbs.

Serves: 4-6

Ingredients	Metric	Imperial
Raw prawns	500 g	1 lb
Sole or flounder fillets	2	2
Squid	500 g	1 lb
Lemons	2	2
Plain flour	3 tablespoons	3 tablespoons
Oil	for deep frying	for deep frying
Batter:		
Self-raising flour	250 ml	1 cup
Brandy	1 tablespoon	1 tablespoon
Oil	1 tablespoon	1 tablespoon
Dried rosemary	½ teaspoon	½ teaspoon
Dried basil	½ teaspoon	½ teaspoon
Salt	¼ teaspoon	¼ teaspoon
Warm water	185 ml	¾ cup
Egg white	1	1

Wash prawns, shell and de-vein. Cut fish fillets into 5 cm (2-inch) long strips. Wash squid under a cold, running tap, remove the ink sac and spine. Peel off skin and cut away eyes. Slice squid into rings, wash again in salted water. Lay prawns, fish and squid flat on a baking tray, sprinkle with the juice of 1 lemon and stand for 3 minutes.

Toss seafood in flour, dip in batter, then fry, a few pieces at a time, in deep hot oil until golden. Drain on crumpled kitchen paper. Arrange on a serving platter and garnish with remaining lemon, cut in wedges. Serve with good mayonnaise flavoured with capers, finely chopped parsley and chopped canned pimiento.

Batter: Sift flour into a bowl. Make a well in the centre, add brandy, oil, herbs and salt. Gradually add water, beating until mixture is smooth. Leave 30 minutes. Just before cooking seafood, whisk egg white until it stands in soft peaks, then very gently fold into the batter. Use immediately.

SQUID

Serves: 4

Ingredients	Metric	Imperial
Squid	750 g	1½ lb
Olive oil	3 tablespoons	3 tablespoons
Salt and pepper	to season	to season

Skin squid, remove head and insides, rub any black lining off with salt, and wash. Cut into several pieces for grilling or into thin slices for pan frying. Place in a dish with oil, salt and pepper to season and let it stand 1 hour turning occasionally.

Pan Fried: Heat a heavy frying pan, drop in squid and cook gently for 3-4 minutes, adding a little more oil if necessary.

Grilled: Place squid under a medium-hot grill and cook 4-5 minutes on each side, brushing occasionally with oil.

In Piquant Sauce: Pan fry squid as above with 3 cloves garlic and half a small hot chilli. When tender, remove garlic and chilli. Combine 1 tablespoon each of breadcrumbs, chopped parsley and butter and toss over squid, stirring over a high heat for 1 minute. Serve with lemon wedges.

BAKED FISH

Pesce al Forna
Serves: 4
Cooking time: 30 minutes
Oven temperature: 170-190°C (350-375°F)

Ingredients	Metric	Imperial
Whole snapper or jewfish	1.125 kg	2¼ lb
Salt and pepper	to season	to season
Onions	2	2
Tomatoes	2	2
Green capsicums	2	2
Butter	125 g	4 oz
Rosemary	1 sprig	1 sprig
Thyme	2-3 sprigs	2-3 sprigs
Bacon rashers	4	4
White wine	125 ml	½ cup

Season inside of cleaned and scaled fish with salt and pepper. Cut 2-3 diagonal slits on both sides of fish, behind gills.

Slice onions and tomatoes, seed and slice capsicums and place some of each in cavity of fish. Add 30 g (1 oz) butter and secure opening with small skewers. Place fish on buttered aluminium foil in a baking dish and rub fish with remaining butter. Season with salt, pepper and add herbs. Lay bacon over top and put remaining sliced vegetables around fish. Bake in a moderate oven for about 30 minutes, basting occasionally with wine and pan juices.

To test if fish is cooked, cut a slit along backbone in the thickest part of the fish (behind head) with the point of a small sharp knife. If flesh is white and flaky, fish is ready.

Note: A good pinch dried rosemary and thyme may replace fresh.

MEAT

MEAT

Italians are very appreciative of the true flavour of meat. They select pork from Romagna, a piece of Tuscan beef, young tender lamb that has not tasted grass, or veal that is only milk fed, often just roasted with butter and a hint of fresh herbs or simply grilled over a charcoal fire.

All over Italy there are regional specialities.

There is osso buco (hollow bone), of Milan. Thick slices of veal shank browned then simmered in wine, herbs and stock. It is served carefully, so that the marrow which is the highlight of the dish stays in the bone, then topped with gremolata, the accepted garnish of lemon rind, chopped garlic and parsley, and accompanied by the golden risotto of Milan, saffron rice.

Another of the specialities of Milan is the cotolet alla Milanese. Tender cutlets of veal are dipped in egg and breadcrumbs and fried until golden brown in olive oil. Veal served Parma style is another dish that is highly praised. This time the veal is topped with slivers of ham from Parma, parmesan cheese and finished off with marsala wine.

In Florence there is beefsteak, just grilled; in Sicily baby lamb, roasted with rosemary and ham; much more is made of the boiled meats in central Italy.

Meat is usually served on its own with perhaps a few potatoes and a side salad — vegetables are served as a separate dish or a first course.

MILANESE VEAL CUTLETS

Cotolete alla Milanese
Serves: 3-4

Ingredients	Metric	Imperial
Veal cutlets	6	6
Milk	to cover	to cover
Eggs, beaten	2	2
Fine dry breadcrumbs	for coating	for coating
Butter	125 g	4 oz
Salt	to season	to season
Lemon wedges for garnish		

Trim cutlets and flatten between 2 sheets of plastic wrap with a meat mallet. With a sharp knife, cut edges of cutlets slightly so they do not curl while cooking. Put cutlets in a large dish and cover with milk. Leave 1 hour — this process whitens and tenderises veal.

Drain cutlets and dry with paper towels. Dip into beaten egg, then coat with breadcrumbs, pressing them on well.

Heat butter in a frying pan. When butter just begins to change colour add cutlets (all at once if using a large pan, or in two lots if pan is small) and cook without moving until golden and crisp on one side. Turn carefully and cook second side until crisp. Lower heat and continue cooking for 5 minutes. Arrange on a warm serving dish and sprinkle with salt. Garnish with lemon wedges.

OSSO BUCO MILANESE

Serves: 4

Ingredients	Metric	Imperial
Butter	30 g	1 oz
Veal shanks, cut in 8 cm (3-inch) pieces	4	4
Plain flour	3 tablespoons	3 tablespoons
Salt	½ teaspoon	½ teaspoon
Pepper	½ teaspoon	½ teaspoon
Dry white wine	250 ml	1 cup
Water	250 ml	1 cup
Tomato paste	1 tablespoon	1 tablespoon
Chopped parsley	1 teaspoon	1 teaspoon
Garlic, chopped	1 clove	1 clove
Lemon rind	1 strip	1 strip
Anchovy fillets, chopped	2	2
Stock	3 tablespoons	3 tablespoons
Extra butter	30 g	1 oz
Gremolata (parsley, garlic and lemon rind) for garnish		

Melt butter in a large deep saucepan. Coat veal pieces lightly with flour. Add a few pieces at a time to pan with salt and pepper and cook until shanks are well browned on all sides. Remove browned pieces from pan and keep warm while browning remaining pieces. Return to pan when all are cooked. Add wine and continue cooking until wine evaporates. Add water and tomato paste, cover and cook over a low heat, adding a little more water when necessary. Baste with liquid every 15 minutes until meat is tender but not falling from the bone, about 1 hour.

Ten minutes before serving, add parsley, garlic, lemon rind and anchovy, cook for 2 minutes, turning shanks over once. Remove lemon rind and place shanks on a warm serving dish. Add stock and butter to pan and mix well into gravy. Pour over veal.

GRILLED SKEWERED PORK FILLET (see page 105)

Serve with gremolata sprinkled over. It is made by combining 3 cloves garlic, chopped; rind of 1 lemon, finely chopped; and 3 tablespoons chopped parsley.

VEAL ESCALOPES PASSETTO

Serves: 4
Cooking time: 10 minutes
Oven temperature: 190-200°C (375-400°F)

Ingredients	Metric	Imperial
Thin veal steaks	4	4
Plain flour	1 tablespoon	1 tablespoon
Prosciutto or ham deluxe	4 slices	4 slices
Mozzarella cheese	4 thin slices	4 thin slices
Dried sage	½ teaspoon	½ teaspoon
Salt and pepper	to season	to season
Butter	for frying	for frying
Grated parmesan cheese	125 ml	½ cup
Extra butter	15 g	½ oz

Sprinkle veal slices with flour then flatten with a meat mallet between 2 sheets of plastic wrap. Place a slice of prosciutto, then cheese on each steak and sprinkle with sage and salt and pepper to taste. Roll up each steak and secure with a cocktail stick.

Heat enough butter in a frying pan to generously cover base. Quickly sauté rolls in two lots, until they are well browned. Place rolls in an ovenproof dish and sprinkle with grated parmesan and a little melted butter. Bake in a moderately hot oven for 10 minutes.

Note: If veal steaks are large, cut each in half and make 8 small rolls, it will be necessary to halve the ham and the cheese.

VEAL WITH HAM AND SAGE

Saltimbocca

Saltimbocca in Italian means 'jump in the mouth'.

Serves: 6

Ingredients	Metric	Imperial
Thin veal steaks	6	6
Prosciutto or ham deluxe	12 slices	12 slices
Fresh sage	12 leaves	12 leaves
Butter	60 g	2 oz
Salt and pepper	to season	to season
Dry white wine	125 ml	½ cup

Cut each steak into 2 even sized pieces. Place between 2 sheets of plastic wrap and·flatten with a wooden meat mallet. Place a thin slice of prosciutto and a safe leaf on each slice of meat and secure with a cocktail stick.

Melt butter in a frying pan, add meat slices and brown quickly on both sides for a few minutes. Add a little salt to taste, remembering that prosciutto adds saltiness of its own, and plenty of freshly ground pepper. Arrange slices of meat, ham side up, on a warm serving dish and keep warm. Add wine (stock or water may be used) to pan and scrape base well, a small hut of butter may be swirled in for a richer sauce. Pour pan gravy over meat.

SICILIAN ROAST LAMB

Agnellino al Forna

As Sicilian lamb is very young and tender, it is usually cooked for only 30 minutes. For older lamb, cook roast for at least 1 hour.

Serves: 6
Cooking time: approximately 1 hour
Oven temperature: 190-200°C (375-400°F)

Ingredients	Metric	Imperial
Leg of lamb	1.5-1.75 kg	3-3½ lb
Prosciutto or bacon, diced	125 g	4 oz
Fresh rosemary	1 sprig	1 sprig
Olive oil	3 tablespoons	3 tablespoons
Salt and pepper	to season	to season
Fresh breadcrumbs	4 tablespoons	4 tablespoons
Grated pecorino or parmesan cheese	4 tablespoons	4 tablespoons

Make small incisions with the point of a knife at regular intervals all over the lamb. Into each incision, insert a piece of prosciutto and a few spikes of rosemary.

Place meat in a roasting pan just large enough to hold it and pour olive oil over. Season with salt and a generous grind of black pepper. Mix breadcrumbs and cheese and sprinkle over meat. Roast in a moderately hot oven for 1 hour or until tender, turning and basting every 20 minutes.

VEAL SCALLOPINE MARSALA

Scaloppine di vitello al marsala
Serves: 4

Ingredients	Metric	Imperial
Very thin veal steaks	4	4
Salt and pepper	to season	to season
Eggs	2	2
Plain flour	3 tablespoons	3 tablespoons
Butter	45 g	1½ oz
Dry marsala or sherry	125 ml	½ cup
Stock, beef consommé or water	125 ml	½ cup

Cut veal steaks in half. Sprinkle with salt and pepper. Dip steaks in beaten eggs. Coat lightly with flour.

Melt 30 g (1 oz) butter in a frying pan (use enough to cover base of pan completely) and brown meat, taking care not to burn, for about 5 minutes on each side. When well browned, add marsala and swirl steaks in liquid so it will thicken itself with the flour and butter. Remove steaks to warm plates.

Add stock and remaining butter to pan, scraping base and sides, swirl to make gravy and pour over meat.

SICILIAN BEEFSTEAK

Bistecchi alla Siciliana
Serves: 4

Ingredients	Metric	Imperial
Tomatoes	4	4
Olive oil	3 tablespoons	3 tablespoons
Garlic	1-2 cloves	1-2 cloves

Fillet steaks	4	4
Chopped black olives	3 tablespoons	3 tablespoons
Sliced sweet pickled capsicums	2 tablespoons	2 tablespoons
Diced celery	2 tablespoons	2 tablespoons
Capers	2-2½ tablespoons	2-2½ tablespoons
Salt and pepper	to season	to season
Chopped fresh oregano	1 teaspoon	1 teaspoon

Peel and chop tomatoes, discarding the seeds. Heat oil in a pan and fry garlic until turning brown. Discard garlic and quickly sear steaks in oil for 2 minutes on each side. Add olives, capsicums, celery, capers and tomato. Season with salt and pepper and sprinkle with oregano. Cook a few minutes longer, then serve at once.

VEAL STEAKS PARMA STYLE

Serves: 4

Ingredients	Metric	Imperial
Veal steaks	4	4
Salt	to season	to season
Plain flour	2 tablespoons	2 tablespoons
Butter	60 g	2 oz
Prosciutto, ham deluxe or ham	125 g	4 oz
Chopped parsley	1 tablespoon	1 tablespoon
Grated parmesan cheese	3 tablespoons	3 tablespoons
Marsala	2 tablespoons	2 tablespoons

Cut each veal steak in 2 regular shapes. Beat lightly with a wooden meat mallet, between 2 sheets of plastic, to flatten. Sprinkle with salt and coat lightly with flour, then fry in butter in a heavy pan until both sides are golden brown, about 6 minutes. If possible, use a frying pan large enough to take them all in one layer. Finely chop ham and mix with parsley and cheese. Divide mixture into 8 portions and put a portion on top of each steak. Sprinkle with marsala and continue cooking for a further 8-10 minutes. Remove from heat and serve immediately with any extra pan gravy spooned over.

VEAL CHOPS PETRONIUS

A noble name for a noble dish. Presumably Petronius could afford the truffle that gives this dish its outstanding flavour. It is still good without the truffle.

Serves: 4

Ingredients	Metric	Imperial
Butter	60 g	2 oz
Veal chops, cut 10 mm (½-inch) thick	4	4
Plain flour	2 tablespoons	2 tablespoons
Marsala or sherry	125 ml	½ cup
Salt	½ teaspoon	½ teaspoon
Chicken stock	125 ml	½ cup
Truffle, finely sliced	1	1
Grated parmesan cheese	4 tablespoons	4 tablespoons

Melt butter in a heavy frying pan. Coat chops lightly with flour and place in the pan. Cook over a high heat for 10 minutes on each side, then add marsala and salt and cook until wine evaporates. Remove chops from pan, add 60 ml (¼ cup) stock and scrape base of pan to loosen all the crustiness. Return chops to pan and on each one place slices of truffle. Sprinkle with parmesan cheese, add remaining stock to pan, cover and cook over a low heat until cheese melts.

PERUGIA ROAST PORK

Arista Perugina

This is the same as Florentine Roast Pork but instead of using rosemary, flavour the pork with fennel leaves and garlic. If fennel leaves are not available, (the top feathery pieces) use the bulbs, finely sliced, and cook the roast on top of the sliced fennel.

PORK WITH MARSALA

Scaloppe di Maiale al Marsala
Serves: 6

Ingredients	Metric	Imperial
Pork fillets	500-750 g	1-1½ lb
Seasoned flour	for coating	for coating
Olive oil	3 tablespoons	3 tablespoons
Salt and freshly ground pepper	to season	to season
Plain flour	2 teaspoons	2 teaspoons
Marsala	125 ml	½ cup
Butter	30 g	1 oz

Trim pork fillets of any fat and slice lengthways, almost through. Lay fillets open, book fashion and flatten with a meat mallet between 2 sheets of plastic wrap. Cut meat into pieces about 10 x 5 cm (4 x 2-inches). Beat again until very thin, taking care not to break the slices. Dust slices lightly with seasoned flour.

Heat oil in a pan and brown meat for 2 minutes on each side over a high heat. Sprinkle lightly with salt and generously with pepper, then remove meat from pan and arrange slices overlapping on a warm serving dish. Keep warm.

Add 1 tablespoon water to pan, then add flour. Stir and pour in marsala, scraping up the crustiness. Stir until sauce is thickened and smooth, then add butter and when melted, pour hot sauce over meat.

FLORENTINE ROAST PORK

Arista Fiorentina
Serves: 6-8
Cooking time: approximately 1¾ hours
Oven temperature: 200-230°C (400-450°F)

Ingredients	Metric	Imperial
Loin of pork	1.75 kg	3½ lb
Fresh rosemary	2 sprigs	2 sprigs
Garlic	3 cloves	3 cloves
Salt and pepper	to season	to season

Ask butcher to chine pork for easier carving, and to slash the pork skin. Make little slits in the meat and insert a spike or two of rosemary and garlic, which has been cut into small slivers. Season with salt and pepper and cook on a spit or in a hot oven for about 1¾ hours, or until meat is tender. Allow to stand for about 20 minutes in a warm place, then slice.

PORK CHOPS MODENA STYLE

Costolette di Maiale alla Modenese
Serves: 4

Ingredients	Metric	Imperial
Pork chops, thickly cut	4	4
Salt and pepper	to season	to season
Chopped rosemary	1 teaspoon	1 teaspoon
Chopped sage	1 teaspoon	1 teaspoon
Garlic, chopped	1 clove	1 clove
Water	125 ml	½ cup
Dry white wine	125 ml	½ cup

Leave fat on pork but slash skin to prevent it from curling while

cooking. Season chops with salt and pepper. Mix herbs and garlic and sprinkle over chops. Lightly grease a heavy pan, add chops and water, cover pan and cook gently over a low heat for about 45 minutes. Turn them occasionally, they will start to brown as the water evaporates.

Remove cover, add wine and cook for a further 5 minutes, turning chops until well browned. Place on a heated serving dish and pour pan gravy over.

GRILLED SKEWERED PORK FILLET

'Lombello' Arrosto

Lombello is the Roman name for fillet of pork.

Serves: 6

Ingredients	Metric	Imperial
Pork fillets	1-1.25 kg	2-2½ lb
Prosciutto or ham	24 thin slices	24 thin slices
Long French loaf	24 slices	24 slices
Oil	4 tablespoons	4 tablespoons
Salt and pepper	to season	to season
Crushed rosemary	1 tablespoon	1 tablespoon

Wipe fillets and remove all fat and skin. Cut into 18 slices, each about the thickness of a finger and all the same size. Cut each slice of prosciutto in half and fold over to the same size as the pieces of pork fillet. On 1 large skewer (or 6 smaller ones), thread a slice of bread, folded prosciutto, pork, another slice of bread, prosciutto etc. until all the ingredients are used.

Drizzle oil over meat and bread. Season with salt, pepper and rosemary and grill over hot coals, or under a hot grill, turning constantly and basting from time to time with oil. Cooking time will be about 30 minutes. Bread should be crisp and golden and meat cooked through. Serve immediately.

FRUIT AND DESSERTS

FRUIT AND DESSERTS

Italian pastry cooks are famous, but the elaborate cakes and desserts they make are reserved for special occasions. In most homes, dessert is most likely to be a choice of cheese and fresh fruit in season, or fruit cooked in a local red or white wine. A dinner table without fruit is hard to find even in the most modest tavern or home.

Then there are the ices and ice creams. They have a fresh light quality, and just the right balance of fruit, sugar and cream so that when frozen, they are not so hard that you bite into them, they just melt in your mouth.

And zabaglione, that most Italian of desserts, a light fluff of sweet creamy wine that is even better when a crisp biscuit is dipped into it or it is served over fresh strawberries.

Fresh flavoured ricotta cheese features in many desserts. One of the simplest is a mixture of ricotta and candied peel, it may be eaten with one of the many little crisp Italian biscuits or used as a filling for tart cases.

One of the most pleasant pastimes in Italy is to sit mid-afternoon with a sweet biscuit or crisp almond cake and an aperitif. The recipe for amaretti is included, try them with a little marsala to get the Italian feeling.

ZUCCOTTO

Serves: 8-10

Ingredients	Metric	Imperial
Sponge cake	28 x 18 cm slab	11 x 7-inch slab
Marsala	4 tablespoons	4 tablespoons
First Layer:		
Cream	250 ml	1 cup
Sugar	60 ml	¼ cup
Vanilla essence	1 teaspoon	1 teaspoon
Chopped candied fruit	125 ml	½ cup
Chocolate Layer:		
Dark cooking chocolate	90 g	3 oz
Hot water	185 ml	¾ cup
Brandy	2 teaspoons	2 teaspoons
Cream	250 ml	1 cup
Strawberry Layer:		
Strawberries	500 ml	2 cups
Cream	250 ml	1 cup
Sugar	60 ml	¼ cup
Red food colouring	few drops	few drops

Line a large deep mould or bowl with strips of sponge cake moistened with marsala. Spoon first layer of filling into bowl and top with chocolate layer, then strawberry layer. Freeze until firm. To serve, unmould on to a plate and cut into wedges.

First Layer: Whip cream with sugar until thick, fold in vanilla essence then candied fruit.

Chocolate Layer: Chop chocolate and place in a bowl with hot water. Stand bowl in hot water until chocolate melts. Stir in brandy, cool. Whip cream and fold in cooled chocolate.

Strawberry Layer: Wash, hull and mash strawberries. Whip cream with sugar, fold in strawberries and enough red food colouring to tint mixture a delicate pink.

APRICOT ICE CREAM

Serves: 4-6

Ingredients	Metric	Imperial
Dried apricots	125 g	4 oz
Cream	315 ml	1¼ cups
Egg yolks	3	3
Sugar	125 ml	½ cup

Cook apricots in a little water until they are tender. Drain and push fruit through a sieve to make a thick pureé. In the top of of a double boiler, gradually stir cream into beaten egg yolks and cook over gently simmering water, stirring constantly, until thickened. Remove custard from heat and add sugar immediately, adding more to taste if necessary, stirring until dissolved. Cool custard, then stir in apricot pureé.

Pour into a deep freezer tray and cover securely with aluminium foil. Freeze until it forms a solid rim about 2.5 cm (1-inch) wide Transfer to a chilled bowl and beat with an electric or rotary beater until smooth. Return to tray and freeze again until firm and creamy.

COFFEE ICE CREAM

Serves: 6

Ingredients	Metric	Imperial
Cream	500 ml	2 cups
Egg yolks	4	4
Freshly roasted coffee beans	250 ml	1 cup
Sugar	185 ml	¾ cup

In the top of a double boiler, gradually stir cream into beaten egg yolks and blend well. Add coffee beans and cook over simmering water, stirring constantly, until thickened. Remove from heat and immediately add sugar, stirring until dissolved. Allow custard to stand several hours to develop a good coffee flavour, then strain through a nylon sieve into a deep freezer tray. Cover tightly with aluminium foil and freeze until it forms a solid rim about 2.5 cm (1-inch) wide. Transfer to a chilled bowl and beat vigorously with an electric or rotary beater. Return to tray and freeze until firm and creamy.

BISCUIT TORTONI

Serves: 8

Ingredients	Metric	Imperial
Finely chopped almonds	165 ml	2/3 cup
Melted butter	1 tablespoon	1 tablespoon
Crushed dry almond macaroons	165 ml	2/3 cup
Cream	500 ml	2 cups
Dark rum	1 tablespoon	1 tablespoon
Sifted icing sugar	85 ml	1/3 cup

Combine almonds and melted butter in an ovenproof dish and toast in a very slow oven 120°C (250°F) stirring every 5 minutes, until nuts are golden. Cool, then combine with macaroon crumbs. Set aside 125 ml (½ cup) of crumb mixture and stir remainder into 125 ml (½ cup) cream and rum. Set aside also.

Beat remaining cream until just thickened, sift in icing sugar and beat until thick. Fold reserved crumb/cream/rum mixture into sweetened whipped cream and pile into 8 small ramekins, doming the mixture. Sprinkle reserved crumb mixture over top and freeze. Remove tortoni from freezer about 5 minutes before serving.

ITALIAN MACAROONS

Amaretti
Makes: 14-16
Cooking time: 15 minutes
Oven temperature: 160-170°C (325-350°F)

Ingredients	Metric	Imperial
Unblanched almonds	335 ml	1¹/₃ cups
Egg whites	2	2
Castor sugar	250 ml	1 cup
Sifted icing sugar	2 tablespoons	2 tablespoons

Blanch almonds in boiling water for 1 minute, then drain and remove skins. Dry out in a barely warm oven, taking care almonds to not colour. Chop, grind or pulverise almonds in an electric blender, to a fine powder.

Beat egg whites until stiff but not dry and fold in almonds and sugar. Pipe mixture on to squares of greaseproof paper in square or oval shapes, about 2.5 cm (1-inch) across. Place on baking trays and dust with icing sugar. Leave aside for 4 hours.

Bake macaroons in a moderately slow oven for 15 minutes or until delicately browned. Remove from oven and allow to cool before removing biscuits from paper squares. Amaretti will keep for some time in an airtight container.

PEARS IN WINE

Serves: 6

Ingredients	Metric	Imperial
Sugar	250 ml	1 cup
Water	125 ml	½ cup
Vanilla pod	1	1
Red or white wine	1 x 410 ml bottle	1 x 13 fl oz bottle
Pears	6-8	6-8
Apricot jam	2 tablespoons	2 tablespoons

Put sugar and water in a saucepan or a deep flameproof casserole and stir over a gentle heat until sugar dissolves. Add vanilla pod which has been split in 2 lengthways and bring to the boil. Reduce heat and add wine.

Peel pears, remove cores from the bottom with a sharp knife and leaving stalks intact.

Place pears in wine and simmer very gently until tender. Turn pears occasionally so that they are covered by the wine at some stage while cooking. They should take about 45 minutes.

The pears may also be cooked in a covered casserole for 1-1½ hours in a moderate oven 170-190°C (350-375°F).

Place pears on a serving plate and pour wine syrup into a small saucepan. Push heated apricot jam through a sieve, add to wine syrup and cook over a high heat until syrup thickens, about 15 minutes. Pour over pears and chill before serving.

ZABAGLIONE

Serves: 4

Ingredients	Metric	Imperial
Egg yolks	8	8
Sugar	2 tablespoons	2 tablespoons
Marsala	315 ml	1¼ cups

Beat egg yolks and sugar together until white in the top of a double boiler. Stir in marsala and place over hot, but not boiling water. Place over a low heat and whisk constantly until mixture is frothy and thick. Take care it does not boil and curdle. As soon as mixture is thick, pour into warmed glasses and serve immediately with crisp biscuits or savoy fingers (sponge fingers) or spoon over ripe strawberries.

SPUMONI ZABAGLIONE

Frozen Zabaglione
Serves: 6-8

Ingredients	Metric	Imperial
Egg yolks	3	3
Water	2 teaspoons	2 teaspoons
Sugar	3 tablespoons	3 tablespoons
Marsala, or similar sweet wine	125 ml	½ cup
Cream	185 ml	¾ cup

Combine egg yolks, water, sugar and wine in the top of a double boiler and whisk over hot, not boiling water until luke-warm. Remove from heat and continue beating until mixture is foamy and slightly thickened. Beat cream until stiff and blend with egg mixture. Pour into a 1 litre (2-pint) mould, cover with aluminium foil and freeze. Cut into wedges to serve.

PEACH AND PLUM COMPOTE

Serves: 6-8

Ingredients	Metric	Imperial
Orange	1 small	1 small
Sugar	375 ml	1½ cups
Water	375 ml	1½ cups
Lemon juice	60 ml	½ cup
Cointreau	2-3 tablespoons	2-3 tablespoons
Ripe peaches	6 large	6 large
Ripe plums	6	6

Peel orange very thinly using a potato peeler, then cut rind into fine strips. In a heavy saucepan, dissolve sugar in water over a gentle heat. Add orange rind strips and boil for 5 minutes. Cool, then add lemon juice and cointreau, according to taste.

Meanwhile, pour boiling water over fruit and allow to stand for about 3 minutes, skin them and put whole into a glass serving bowl. Pour syrup over fruit, cover top of bowl securely with clear plastic wrap or aluminium foil and chill.

RICOTTA TARTS

Makes: 12-14 tarts
Cooking time: 10 minutes
Oven temperature: 200-230ºC (400-450ºF)

Ingredients	Metric	Imperial
Pastry:		
Plain flour	500 ml	2 cups
Butter	125 g	4 oz
Castor sugar	125 ml	½ cup
Egg	1	1
Egg yolk	1	1
Salt	pinch	pinch
Filling:		
Ricotta cheese	500 g	1 lb
Sugar	125 ml	½ cup
Mixed candied orange and lemon peel	125 ml	½ cup

Pastry: Sift flour into a bowl, rub in butter. Add sugar, then lightly beaten egg and egg yolk, and salt. Mix into a ball but do not knead. Wrap in clear plastic and chill for 1 hour. Roll out thinly and cut into rounds to fit small greased tartlet tins. Chill 10-15 minutes. Prick well with a fork and bake in a hot oven for 8-10 minutes or until golden. Cool. Just before serving, spoon ricotta filling into tarts.

Filling: Mix ricotta cheese with sugar and chopped peel.

SHORT GLOSSARY OF SOME CONTINENTAL TERMS

Agneau: Lamb.

Amandes: Almonds.

Américaine: (à l') Dishes cooked with tomato and herbs.

Anglaise: (à l') Dishes cooked in water.

Artichaut: (fonds d') Artichoke hearts.

Asperges: Asparagus.

Aspic: Meat, game or fish glaze jelly.

Aubergine: Eggplant.

Béarnaise: Sauce of egg yolks, shallots and tarragon vinegar.

Bordelaise: (à la) Sauce of wine and marrow.

Bouillabaisse: A Provençale fish soup.

Boulangère: (à la) Garnish of thinly sliced potatoes and/or onions.

Bourgignonne: (à la) Meat cooked in wine with a garnish of bacon.

Canapés: Small pieces of bread or toast upon which is placed a mouthful of tasty food.

Caneton: Duckling.

Cardinal: Lobster sauce and garnish.

Carpet Bag Steak: A thick piece of rump steak stuffed with oysters.

Champignon: Mushroom.

Chantilly, Crème: Whipped cream.

Chasseur: (à la) Garnish of mushrooms and shallots cooked in white wine.

Châteaubriand: A thick steak from the middle of the fillet.

Consommé: Clear soup.

Coq: Cockerel.

Crème: Cream and/or a thick creamy soup.

Crêpes: Thin pancakes.

Croquettes: Crisp, fried balls of various foods.

Croûte: (En croûte) Crust. A pie.

Diable: (à la) Devilled or highly spiced.

Entrecôte: Sirloin steak.

Escalope: Flattened slice of meat, fried.

Espagnole: A basic brown sauce from which many other sauces are made.

Filet Mignon: A piece of steak cut from the fillet.

Flamande: (à la) Garnish of braized cabbage, carrots, pork and potatoes.

Flambé: To pour brandy or fortified wine over food and ignite.

Florentine: (à la) Denotes spinach.

Foie Gras: Made from goose or duck liver.

Fraises: Strawberries.

Française: (à la) Duchesse potatoes filled with mixed vegetables, asparagus tips, cauliflower, braized lettuce.

Fromage: Cheese.

Gâteau: Cake.

Gratin, Gratiné: The crust formed from browning in an oven or under a grill.

Hollandaise: Hot sauce made with yolks of eggs and butter.

Hors d'Oeuvre: A selection of hot or cold dishes served as a preliminary to a meal.

Huîtres: Oysters.

Italienne: (à l') Dishes with chopped mushrooms.

Jambon: Ham.

Julienne: Fresh vegetables cut up finely for soups or garnishes.

Kebab, Shish Kebab, Shashlik: Small pieces of marinated meat threaded on skewers and grilled.

Kirsch: A liqueur distilled from wild cherries.

Lapin: Rabbit.

Marengo: A chicken dish said to have been invented by Napoleon's chef. The dish traditionally includes fried eggs and is garnished with crayfish.

Marron: Chestnut.

Meunière: (à la) Fish fried in butter.

Mornay: Sauce made from béchamel sauce, cream, parmesan or gruyère cheese.

Mousse: Light sweet or savoury, whipped with whites of eggs.

Newburg: A method of preparing shellfish which is served in a rich sauce of butter, cream, sherry and egg yolks.

Niçoise: (à la) Denotes tomatoes.

Noisettes d'Agneau: Small round slices from the cutlet or saddle of lamb.

Normande: (à la) Poultry or meat cooked in cider and cream.

Pâté: A very fine savoury mixture made from liver, pork, game and served cold, generally as an hors d'oeuvre.

Paupiettes: Thin slices of stuffed rolled meat wrapped in bacon.

Petits Pois: Green peas.

Petits Fours: Small fancy cakes and biscuits.

Poisson: Fish.

Poivre: Pepper.

Pomme de Terre: Potato.

Portugaise: (à la) Tomato 'fondue' with onion and garlic.

Potage: Soup.

Poulet: Chicken.

Poussin: Baby chicken.

Praliné: Almond flavoured.

Ragoût: A brown stew of meat or poultry.

Ratatouille: Eggplant, zucchini, onions, tomatoes and capsicums cooked in olive oil.

Rollmops: Rolled pickled herrings filled with onions.

Rôti: Roast.

Roulade: Rolled piece of meat.

Sauerkraut: Pickled white cabbage.

Sauté: Tossed in fat or butter.

Soubise: Accompaniment of onions.

Suprème: A creamy white sauce made with chicken stock. Boned and skinned wing of chicken.

Tartare: Mayonnaise sauce with egg yolks and chives or raw fillet of beef with a raw egg yolk.

Torte: Cake.

Tournedos: Small pieces of the heart of a fillet of beef.

Vinaigrette: A spicy dressing of oil, vinegar, chopped shallots, gherkins and capers.

Vol-au-Vent: A small puff pastry case filled with any suitable food.

Weiner Schnitzel: Thin pieces of veal or pork dipped in flour, egg and breadcrumbs and fried in fat.

Zabaglione: Italian sweet, light and foamy. Made with egg yolks, sugar and marsala.

117

GLOSSARY

Al dente (ahl DEN-tay) 'to the tooth'. Term used to indicate macaroni products which are not overcooked.

Amaretti (ah-mar-ET-tee) — 'little bitter ones' (from amaro, 'Bitter'). Macaroons, usually made with almond meal.

Antipasto (ahn-tee-PAH-sto) 'before meal'. General term used for appetizers or hors d'oeuvre.

Arista (AH-rees-tah) — pork loin or back.

Basilico (bah-SEE-lee-ko) — sweet basil, a herb, derived from the Greek basilikos 'kingly', 'royal'.

Buon gusto (bwon GOOS-toe) — 'good taste'.

Burro e parmigiano (BOOR-roe ay par-me-JAH-no) — 'butter and parmesan cheese'. Macaroni is often eaten plain, with only these two seasonings.

Cacciatora (kah-chyah-TOE-rah) — 'hunter style'.

Cannelloni (kay-nay-LO-nee) — 'big pipes'. A large round macaroni product, usually filled with meat or other ingredients.

Crostino (crust-EE-no) — from crosta, 'crust'. Bread that is spread with anything and then toasted.

Fritto misto (FREE-toe MEES-toe) — mixed fry.

Gnocchi (NYOK-kee) — dumplings made of flour, potatoes or semolina.

Lasagne (lay-SAY-nyay) — giant noodles, over an inch wide, usually baked in the oven (after boiling) with meat or cheese and sauce.

Marinara (mah-ree-NAH-rah) — 'sailor', 'sailor-style'.

Marsala (mar-SAH-lah) — a heavy, semi-sweet dessert wine, produced in Sicily and named after the city of Marsala.

Minestrone (mee-nest-ROE-nay) — 'big soup' from minestra, 'soup'. A thick vegetable soup.

Mozzarella (mo-tsah-REL-lah) — a fresh cheese.

Oregano (aw-RAY-gah-no) — the herb used in many Italian dishes.

Ossobuco (aw-so-BOO-ko) — 'hollow-bone'. A speciality of Milan made from veal shanks.

Parmigiana (par-mee-JAH-nah) — Parma style. Parma is a city in northern Itaiy. Parmesan cheese is parmigiano.

Pasta (PAHS-tah) — dough. Also a generic name for all macaroni products. Not to be confused with the English word 'paste'.

Pizza (PEE-tsah) — 'pie' 'tart'. Generic term for any bakery product that is flat and round.

Prosciutto (pro-SHOOT-toe) — Ham, prepared Italian style. (dried, salted, spiced and pressed, but not sugar-cured or smoked).

Ricotta (ree-KUT-tah) — 're-cooked', 'cooked again'. A substance not unlike cottage cheese, obtained by the repeated boiling of skimmed milk.

Ripieno (ree-PYAY-no) — as an adjective: 'stuffed', as a noun: 'stuffing'.

Risotto (ree-SUT-toe) — 'big rice'. Boiled rice, with a sauce, much favoured in the northern regions of Italy.

Salame (sah-LAH-may). From the root of sale, 'salt'. A salted and spiced pork product, to be eaten sliced. Salami is the plural form and means several pieces of salame.

Saltimbocca (sahl-teem-BO-kah) 'jump into the mouth'. The name of a tasty Roman dish which is so good that it figuratively jumps into the mouth of its own accord.

Scalloppine (skal-lo-PEE-nay) — thin slices of meat (usually veal) stewed or fried.

Spaghetti (spah-GET-tee) — from spago 'cord'. The thinner varieties of macaroni products.

Stracciatella (strah-chah-TEL-lah) — 'little ragged' (from stracci 'rags'). The Roman egg soup, in which flaked eggs resemble tiny fragments of rag.

Zabaione (sah-bah-yo-nay) — a fluffy, light dessert of egg yolks, sugar and wine, served hot or cold. Also known as zabaglione.

INDEX